Daniel Hart

The Book of COMMON SENSE

50 Timeless Rules for a Better Life

Copyright

The Book of Common Sense
© 2025 by Daniel Hart

All rights reserved.

No part of this book may be reproduced, distributed, or transmitted in any form or by any means, including photocopying, recording, or other electronic or mechanical methods, without the prior written permission of the publisher, except in the case of brief quotations embodied in critical reviews and certain other non-commercial uses permitted by copyright law.

ISBN: 978-1-0697533-0-4

Published by Northwind Publishing

Cover design by Northwind Publishing

This is a work of nonfiction. The advice and opinions expressed are those of the author. While every effort has been made to ensure accuracy, the author and publisher assume no responsibility for errors or omissions, or for any consequences resulting from the use of the information contained herein.

The information provided is for general guidance and does not constitute professional, legal, medical, or financial advice. Neither the author nor the publisher shall be held liable for any damages resulting from the application of the information contained in this book.

First Edition

For everyone who showed me that common sense lives in everyday choices.

Table of Contents

INTRODUCTION..1

1. MINDSET AND PERSPECTIVE..7

   YOU ARE NOT THE CENTER OF THE UNIVERSE.............................9
   CHOOSE A BETTER ATTITUDE...13
   THE WORLD OWES YOU NOTHING..18
   NO ONE IS THINKING ABOUT YOU AS MUCH AS YOU THINK THEY ARE..........23
   YOU CAN'T CONTROL OTHERS, JUST YOUR RESPONSE..................29
   DISCIPLINE BEATS MOTIVATION..34
   CONFIDENCE IS QUIET, INSECURITY IS LOUD.................................40
   YOU DON'T NEED A REASON TO DO THE RIGHT THING..................45
   DON'T MAKE PERMANENT DECISIONS BASED ON TEMPORARY EMOTIONS..........50
   BETTER LATE THAN NEVER...55

2. EVERYDAY HABITS...59

   LEAVE FIVE MINUTES EARLIER..61
   GO TO BED EARLIER..66
   SAY NO MORE OFTEN...71
   DON'T ARGUE WITH PEOPLE LOOKING FOR A FIGHT......................76
   DON'T PUT OFF WHAT TAKES LESS THAN TWO MINUTES................81
   MAKE FEWER PROMISES AND KEEP THEM ALL................................86
   LEAVE SPACES BETTER THAN YOU FOUND THEM............................91
   WRITE IT DOWN: MEMORY IS UNRELIABLE......................................96
   START SMALL, BUT START..101
   TAKE CARE OF THINGS THAT TAKE CARE OF YOU..........................107

3. PEOPLE AND RELATIONSHIPS...113

   BE KINDER THAN NECESSARY: PEOPLE ARE FIGHTING BATTLES YOU CAN'T SEE..........115
   YOU TEACH PEOPLE HOW TO TREAT YOU.....................................120
   DON'T INTERRUPT..125
   SAY WHAT YOU MEAN, BUT DON'T SAY IT MEAN..........................130
   LISTEN MORE THAN YOU TALK...136
   APOLOGIZE WHEN YOU'RE WRONG: IT'S STRENGTH, NOT WEAKNESS..........142
   NEVER BURN BRIDGES UNLESS YOU'RE ABSOLUTELY SURE..........147
   DON'T TRY TO WIN ARGUMENTS. TRY TO SOLVE PROBLEMS........152
   SURROUND YOURSELF WITH PEOPLE WHO MAKE YOU BETTER......157
   TREAT PEOPLE BETTER THAN THEY TREAT YOU (BUT DON'T BE A DOORMAT)............162

4. TOOLS FOR LIFE 167

LEARN HOW TO COOK A FEW MEALS WELL 169
LEARN BASIC FIRST AID 174
DON'T POST IN ANGER 179
CHECK THE SOURCE BEFORE SHARING 184
ASK QUESTIONS WHEN YOU DON'T UNDERSTAND 188
READ THE INSTRUCTIONS 193
BEING BUSY ≠ BEING PRODUCTIVE 198
YOUR PHONE IS A TOOL, NOT A LEASH 204
YOU DON'T NEED TO RESPOND RIGHT AWAY 209
REPUTATION IS LIKE GLASS: EASY TO BREAK, HARD TO FIX 214

5. KEEP GROWING 221

STAY CURIOUS 223
READ BEYOND YOUR INTERESTS 229
LEARN BY DOING 234
PRACTICE UNTIL IT'S NATURAL 239
CONNECT THE DOTS 245
SEEK FEEDBACK INSTEAD OF PRAISE 251
TEACH WHAT YOU KNOW 256
LOOK BACK TO MOVE FORWARD 261
DON'T BE AFRAID OF MAKING MISTAKES 266
DON'T GET COMFORTABLE 271

BEFORE YOU GO 277

Introduction

Introduction

You know those moments when you do something and immediately think, *I knew better than that?*

You open your mouth and say something you wish you could take back.

You agree to something you did not want to do, just to avoid an awkward moment.

You put something off even though you had plenty of time to get it done.

We all have those moments. We all know better, at least in theory. But knowing and doing are two very different things.

We all like to think we have common sense. And in most cases, we probably do. But life has a way of distracting us. We get caught up in deadlines, obligations, small frustrations, and big plans. We focus on what is urgent instead of what is important. In the process, we forget the simplest things that could make life easier, kinder, and a little more balanced.

That is what this book is about. Not a lecture. Not a manual. Not philosophy. Not complicated theories or life hacks that require a complete overhaul of your routines. It is about the small, practical truths that you already know but might need to hear again. The habits that make things work better. The perspective shifts that make the day feel lighter. The tiny actions that, if you keep repeating them, quietly change the way life feels.

The ideas in this book are not new. They are not a complete list of everything that matters. You have probably heard many of them from a parent, a friend, a coach, or even a stranger at some point. Some you might already practice without thinking. Others you might have forgotten about, or let slide without meaning to. And some will probably make you say: *I know this. Why am I not doing it?*

I have asked myself the same thing many times over the years. That

Introduction

question stayed with me. Over the years, I kept noticing how often people acted in ways that went against common sense. Sometimes it was small choices. Sometimes it was big ones. And often enough, I caught myself doing the same.

I pictured this book for almost twenty years. I thought about how I would organize it, the stories I would tell, and the lessons I would include. And then I did nothing. Year after year, the idea stayed in the back of my mind but never made it to the page.

What finally pushed me forward was noticing how often the same simple truths kept showing up in my own life. I would forget them, relearn them, and then watch the people around me stumble over them too. It became clear that the world did not need more clever ideas. It needed reminders.

So I sat down and began writing. Not because I had mastered these principles, but because I needed them as much as anyone else. Writing them down helped me see my own thinking more clearly. It reminded me where I still get in my own way and where I need to practice what I already know.

If anyone else finds something useful in these pages, that is a bonus. That is a win-win.

I am not here to pretend I have always practiced what I preach. Far from it. I have overlooked my better judgment more times than I can count. I have delayed things I knew needed to be done. I have spoken when silence would have served me better. I have stayed up long past the hour I should have slept. I have stepped into arguments I never needed to join. I have ignored the obvious step that would have saved me trouble. And I have told myself I was too busy for the very things that would have made life easier.

That is why this book exists. It is a reminder, for me as much as for you.

The pages ahead are not rules carved in stone. They are invitations. They are nudges. They are tools. They are simple, repeatable

Introduction

actions you can use to get back on track when life gets messy. They are ways to steady yourself, improve your relationships, protect your time, and take better care of your energy. They are the things you already know deep down, but might need to hear at the right moment.

The ideas in this book are loosely grouped into categories such as Mindset and Perspective, Everyday Habits, People and Relationships, Tools for Life, and Keep Growing. These labels are simply there to make the book easier to navigate. Life itself does not fit neatly into boxes. A habit that improves your health might also strengthen your relationships. A mindset shift that helps you at work might also make you a better friend. The same piece of advice can apply to your job, your friendships, your health, and your sanity, often in ways you do not expect until you put it into practice.

You can read this book from start to finish, letting one idea lead naturally into the next. But you don't have to.

You can open it anywhere, skip to the chapter that speaks to you, or go straight to the section that feels most relevant in the moment. The advice is meant to stand on its own, so you can use it however it fits best into your life. You may even find it best to move slowly, reading just one or two sections a day so the ideas have time to settle before you turn the page.

While reading, you will probably stop more than once and think: *But I know this. This is nothing new.* And you would be right. That is the point. This is not rocket science. It is common sense. The kind you already have, but sometimes need to be reminded to use.

None of this is about being perfect. Perfection is not the goal.

It is about being a little better than you were yesterday. It is about noticing when you slip into habits that do not serve you. It is about making small course corrections before you drift too far. Even the smallest adjustment can change the way a day unfolds.

Catch the little things before they grow into big problems. Keep making those small changes, and they will shape the way life feels. One day you will look back and realize that those small changes were not small at all.

If you try even a few of these ideas, you might notice small problems staying small because you catch them early. You might find yourself having easier conversations, handling situations with a little more patience, and feeling steadier when life throws you a curveball.

You do not need to overhaul your life to make progress. One small, practical step is enough to start.

Tonight, choose one tiny action you can actually do tomorrow morning. Listen more than you talk. Seek feedback instead of praise. Don't argue with people looking for a fight. Apologize when you're wrong.

So tonight, write it down so you do not forget. Then tomorrow, read it and do it. And then choose another step. Then do it. Stay curious. Don't post in anger. Go to bed a little earlier.

At the end of each day, ask yourself, "What simple thing did I do today that will make tomorrow easier?" Jot it down. Appreciate that win. Then repeat.

You might be surprised at how these little efforts add up. Before long, your days feel steadier. Your relationships warmer. Your mind clearer. And all without dramatic changes or complicated tricks.

So choose that one small action.

Put it on your list. Do it tomorrow.

Then keep going, one step at a time.

Your future self will thank you.

That is common sense.

PART ONE

Mindset and Perspective

Mindset and Perspective

How you see the world shapes how you move through it. If you think life owes you, you will stay disappointed. If you believe everyone is watching, you will hold back. The truth is simpler. Most people are too busy with their own lives, and the world owes you nothing. What you can control is your attitude and your response. This chapter is about choosing steadiness over drama and remembering that storms will come, but your balance matters more than the storm.

You Are Not the Center of the Universe

Somewhere along the way, the world started telling people they were the main character. That their story mattered more than everyone else's. That their dreams should take priority. That their time was too valuable to waste. That their feelings were the most valid. That their version of the truth was the one that counted.

That everything should revolve around their goals. Their time. Their truth. And that anyone who got in the way was either a problem or an afterthought.

But you are not the main character in everyone else's story. Other people are not here to serve your timeline, your needs, or your moods.

They are not obstacles to get around or extras in the background of your day. They are living their own lives, with the same complexity, urgency, and emotion that you feel in yours.

When you stop putting yourself at the center, you stop feeling the pressure to control everything. You do not need to win every argument. You do not need to make every plan go your way. You do not need to convince everyone to agree with you. The world does not hinge on your preferences. That truth is freeing.

Think about the last time someone cut you off in traffic. Did they do it because they hate you? No. They did it because they were thinking only about themselves. Their urgency mattered more in their mind. It was not personal.

Most things are not personal.

The friend who forgot to text back was probably distracted. The coworker who seemed rushed might have had a rough morning. The cashier who did not smile may have been exhausted.

Mindset and Perspective

It is rarely about you. And the more you remember that, the less defensive and resentful you become.

This awareness changes the way you move through the world. Instead of rushing to demand better treatment, you pause. Instead of assuming the worst, you give people the benefit of the doubt. Instead of taking offense at everything, you recognize that everyone is carrying a load you cannot see.

And when you do that, you create space for kindness.

The best leaders understand this. They do not assume the spotlight should be fixed on them. They know their role is to bring out the best in others, not to make everything about themselves.

The best friends understand this. They ask questions. They listen. They celebrate your wins without making them about their own.

The best partners understand this. They balance their needs with yours. They compromise. They share the load.

Notice that none of these examples involves erasing yourself. Humility is not self-erasure. It is self-awareness. It is knowing you matter, while also knowing others matter too.

Ego-centrics often confuse humility with weakness. They think stepping back means being overlooked. But the opposite is true. When you live with humility, people notice. They feel respected. They feel valued. They remember how you made them feel. And they trust you more.

Contrast that with someone who always has to dominate the room. People may listen to them out of obligation, but rarely out of loyalty. Attention can be demanded, but respect has to be earned.

The point is not to think less of yourself. The point is to think of yourself less often. To step outside your own head and pay attention to the people around you. Notice their expressions. Notice their tone. Notice their needs instead of assuming yours should always come first.

It means lifting your eyes from your own reflection and remembering that there is a whole world moving around you. People are rushing, struggling, celebrating, and hoping, just like you are. When you let that reality sink in, it becomes harder to walk through life as if your problems and plans are the only ones that matter.

And when you carry that awareness, the weight of being the center slips away. You stop trying to bend every conversation back to yourself. You stop forcing your opinion to be the loudest. You stop demanding that every detail bend to your preference. You learn to relax into the truth that life works better when space is shared.

Of course, you will slip. Everyone does. Pride creeps in. Frustration takes over. You find yourself acting like the center again, expecting people to move around your mood, your schedule, your opinion.

But the moment you notice it, you have a choice. You can pause. You can step aside. You can remind yourself that the world is full of lives just as vivid, just as demanding, and just as important as your own.

This does not just change how others experience you. It changes how you experience life. When you stop insisting that everything revolves around you, the world feels less like an opponent and more like a shared space. Instead of clashing with everyone else's priorities, you learn to adjust to them. Instead of competing for attention, you learn to give it.

And strangely enough, when you give more, you usually receive more in return. Respect. Patience. Grace.

That shift changes how you see your place in the world.

You are not the center of the universe. That is not an insult. It is a gift. It means the world is not waiting on your approval to keep spinning.

Mindset and Perspective

Life moves forward whether you agree with it or not. The sun rises without your permission. Seasons change without checking your schedule. People live, love, struggle, and grow without needing your sign-off. That may bruise the ego at first, but it is also freeing.

It means you can breathe. You do not need to carry every burden or fix every detail. You do not need to be the loudest voice or the final word. The weight of holding everything together was never meant for one person. Letting go of that pressure gives you space to rest.

And it means you can share space generously instead of fighting for it. You can let someone else have the spotlight without losing your own worth. You can make room for another person's idea, another person's success, another person's need, without it diminishing you. There is enough room in the world for more than one story at a time.

When you stop trying to be the center of the universe, you finally see the beauty of being part of it.

You realize the value is not in rising above others, but in walking beside them.

Life grows richer when it is shared.

Life is brighter when it is not all about you.

And far more alive when you remember you are one voice in a greater chorus.

That is common sense.

Choose a Better Attitude

Your attitude is one of the few things in life that you can always control.

Not your circumstances. Not what other people say. Not the mood of the room, or the headlines, or the weather, or the day you woke up to. But your attitude, the way you meet all those things, is yours. Fully yours.

That is both liberating and inconvenient. Because it means you can no longer blame everything around you for the way you carry yourself. You do not get to say, "Well, the day started badly, so of course I'm in a mood." You do not get to put your bitterness on someone else's plate just because your morning felt off. You can. But you don't have to.

Choosing a better attitude is not about pretending everything is fine.

It is not about putting on a fake smile or acting like nothing is wrong. It is not about covering up how you feel or forcing yourself to be cheerful when you are not.

It is not about smiling through pain or ignoring your real emotions. It is not about pushing feelings aside or pretending they do not exist. Your emotions are real, and they deserve to be acknowledged, not hidden.

It is about deciding how you want to move through life, regardless of the circumstances. About choosing the way you carry yourself, even when the situation around you is difficult. About holding on to your sense of self, even when things are not going your way.

Even when it's hard. Especially when it's hard. Those are the moments when your attitude makes the biggest difference.

Mindset and Perspective

Because how you show up affects how things unfold. Not always in big, dramatic ways. Sometimes in subtle ones. In how people respond to you. In how you respond to them. In how you handle setbacks, annoyances, delays, and stress. Your attitude shapes the energy you bring into every moment. And over time, that energy shapes your experience of life.

A negative attitude narrows your view.

It shrinks everything down to what's wrong, what's annoying, what's unfair. You start to expect the worst, and then, because your attention is glued to it, you find it. You see rudeness where there might have been a misunderstanding. You assume judgment where there might have been silence. You treat challenges like personal attacks. You start to think the world is out to get you, or at least in your way.

That way of thinking builds on itself. It becomes your filter. You carry it into traffic. Into the store. Into work. Into your home. And slowly, you stop seeing people as individuals. You see them as problems. As interruptions. As annoyances. Even the good moments feel dull, like they do not land the way they should. Nothing feels like enough. You are always irritated. Always waiting for the next thing to go wrong.

That kind of attitude does not stay contained. It spills. Into your tone. Into your posture. Into your relationships. People feel it. Even when you don't say it out loud. And they start reacting to you based on what you're giving off, which only reinforces your sense that everyone is difficult and everything is a battle.

But here is the hard truth. It is not always the situation. Sometimes, it is your attitude that needs to change.

You are not powerless. Even if the morning started badly. Even if things are already off track. You still have a say in how the rest of the day goes. You still have choices.

You are not at the mercy of the day. The events around you do not get to decide your attitude. The interruptions, the delays, the stress. They do not have to control how you show up.

You are not stuck with the mood you woke up in.

Just because you felt one way when you opened your eyes does not mean you have to carry that feeling with you. Moods shift. Energy changes. You are allowed to reset.

You can shift.

The shift starts with awareness. Paying attention to what you are bringing into a room. Not what others are doing. Not what went wrong that morning. But what *you* are adding to the space. Are you making things heavier or lighter? More tense, or more relaxed? Are you part of the stress, or part of the steadiness?

That doesn't mean you never get to feel tired or upset or disappointed. It means you don't let those things run the whole show.

You don't have to deny your feelings. But you do have to decide which ones you are going to feed.

A better attitude starts small. It starts with a breath. With a pause before speaking. With choosing not to snap, even when it would feel good for a second. It starts with looking someone in the eye instead of brushing them off. With saying thank you and meaning it. With letting one small thing go instead of letting it ruin your whole morning.

And no, that doesn't solve everything. But it changes something. It changes *you*. And that's where most change begins.

Your attitude affects how you handle stress. It affects how you bounce back from setbacks. It affects how others experience you.

If you walk through life bitter, people will start to avoid you. Not because they are mean, but because being near you feels like walking through a storm they didn't sign up for. That is not

Mindset and Perspective

judgment. That is human nature.

But if you carry yourself with steadiness, with grace, with a little humor, even when things are off, people notice. They feel it. They sense the calm in you, the steadiness in your tone, the way you are not shaken by every small disruption. It puts them at ease.

When you have a good attitude people feel safer around you. They know they will not be met with tension or sharpness. They know you are not looking for a fight or waiting to snap. Your presence becomes something steady they can lean on, even if just a little.

You feel better within yourself. You are not constantly reacting. You are not letting every inconvenience set the tone. You move through the day with more clarity, more control, more peace. You carry yourself the way you want to feel, and eventually, you start to feel that way too.

Some people hear this and think it means you have to be fake. That you have to pretend everything is great when it's not. But choosing a better attitude does not mean forcing positivity. It means you do not let a bad moment dictate the rest of the day. It means you notice when your mindset is making things worse, and you gently course-correct.

It means you take responsibility for your tone. For your reactions. For the stories you tell yourself about what is happening.

Instead of saying, "This always happens to me," you ask, "How do I want to respond to this right now?"

That shift is everything.

It moves you from the sidelines into the game.

You cannot control every outcome.

But you can control the energy you bring to the moment. You can decide to stay calm. To be kind. To reset when you need to. You can decide not to take everything so personally. You can learn to laugh more, to pause more, to take things less seriously when the moment allows.

And the more you do that, the easier it gets. The more natural it becomes. Your attitude becomes less reactive and more grounded. Less about the noise around you, and more about the tone you set within you.

That becomes your baseline. Not fake joy. Not forced positivity. Just a balanced presence.

It is a decision to meet life with strength, not complaint.

Because the way you think shapes the way you move. And the way you move shapes how people respond. And how they respond shapes how your day unfolds.

So if you want to change how the day feels, start with your attitude.

Not because it will fix everything. But because it will help you face it all with more strength, more clarity, and more grace.

That is common sense.

The World Owes You Nothing

You've probably heard the phrase before.

Maybe from a frustrated parent. Maybe from a stern teacher. Maybe from a boss who thought you were asking for too much. It can sound harsh. Cold, even. Like a slap of reality wrapped in tough love.

But underneath the sharpness, there's a truth worth hearing.

The world does not owe you anything.

Not a job. Not recognition. Not love. Not success. Not praise. Not understanding. Not even fairness.

It is not personal. It is just reality.

That does not mean your feelings don't matter. It does not mean injustice is okay or that you shouldn't fight for what's right. It simply means this: the world does not rearrange itself based on what you think you deserve. It does not hand out rewards just because you showed up. Life isn't a vending machine where you insert effort and automatically get results.

You can do everything "right" and still hit a wall.

You can work hard and not get the promotion. Be kind and still be misunderstood. Show up and still get overlooked. That's not failure. That's not proof you're doing something wrong. It is just how life works sometimes. Unpredictable. Unfair. Imperfect.

If you expect the world to treat you like it owes you something, you will spend a lot of time bitter, disappointed, and stuck.

Because this is what happens. You start measuring your worth based on what you think you should be getting. You tell yourself that because you worked hard, people should notice. Because you were kind, people should return the favor. Because you have struggled, life should cut you a break. And when that does not happen, when the recognition does not come, when the help is not offered, when life stays hard longer than it feels like it should, you start to feel resentful.

Not just at the world. But at people. At friends. At coworkers. At strangers who seem to have it easier. You start to feel overlooked. Undervalued. Invisible. And over time, that frustration builds. It hardens. That frustration slowly hardens into a bitterness that seeps into everything. You stop celebrating other people's success because it feels like proof that you've been left behind. You stop enjoying the small wins because you're too focused on the reward you didn't get.

And that mindset? It doesn't help you move forward. It keeps you stuck. It turns you inward. It drains your energy, your motivation, and your sense of purpose. Because instead of pouring yourself into the work, the growth, the moment, you're waiting. For someone to notice. For someone to validate you. For life to finally be "fair."

But fairness isn't a finish line. And waiting isn't a strategy.

Now here's the good news.

Once you let go of the idea that something is owed to you, everything changes.

You stop waiting. You stop keeping score. You stop looking around thinking, "When is it going to be my turn?" You start creating. Building. Growing. You take responsibility for your path instead of resenting the one you weren't handed. You start playing the long game.

Because here's the truth most people don't say out loud: entitlement keeps you small.

It convinces you that your current situation is someone else's fault.

That your happiness is being blocked by things outside your control. That if you want something badly enough, it should just show up. That effort guarantees reward. That life is supposed to be fair. And when it's not, the world is to blame.

You start waiting for someone to notice, to help, to fix it. But that kind of thinking strips you of your power. It keeps you focused on what you lack instead of what you can do. It feels justified. But it quietly keeps you stuck.

But that's not how it works.

Wanting something is easy. Working for it, without guarantees, is the real test.

And no, that doesn't mean you have to hustle yourself into burnout. It doesn't mean grinding nonstop or pretending you don't care when life knocks you down. It just means showing up, again and again, even when it's not fair. Even when it's not easy. Even when you feel like you "shouldn't have to."

That's maturity. That's resilience.

You start showing up not because the world owes you something, but because you've decided to owe it to yourself.

You owe yourself the chance to try.

You owe yourself the dignity of effort.

You owe yourself the respect of showing up for yourself, even when no one else sees it.

When you shift your mindset from "I deserve this" to "I'll earn this," something clicks. You stop being a passenger and start being the driver. You stop waiting for the right time, the right conditions, the right approval. You just begin.

And slowly, quietly, things shift.

You build confidence. Not because someone handed it to you, but because you earned it. Through failure. Through learning. Through repetition. You stop needing constant praise because you've started trusting your own growth. You've started seeing yourself as someone who can figure it out.

But let's be clear: this isn't about accepting injustice or staying quiet when you're being mistreated.

Knowing the world owes you nothing does not mean putting up with nonsense.

You can still expect to be treated with decency. You can still speak up. Still ask for what you need. Still advocate for yourself and others. You can still believe in equity and fairness and human dignity.

You just stop waiting for the world to hand it to you.

You stop assuming that just because you are a good person, good things will follow. You stop building your expectations on invisible promises that were never made.

This shift isn't about lowering your standards. It is about raising your ownership of what happens next.

It is about realizing that no one is coming to rescue you. That no one has the perfect plan for your life. That the sooner you stop waiting for someone else to validate your existence, the freer you become.

Because when you take full ownership of your life, not just the wins, but the responsibility, you start to feel powerful. Not in a loud, controlling way. In a quiet, grounded, clear way.

You realize you don't need the world to owe you.

Because you are already in motion. You are already building something. You are already becoming the kind of person who does not wait for permission. You give yourself the green light.

Mindset and Perspective

That's the shift.

And that's when doors start to open. Not always right away. Not always the way you expected. But steadily. Over time. Because people are drawn to those who own their path. Who carry themselves with humility and grit. Who show up not because it's easy, but because it matters.

There's a strength in that.

And here's the other side of it: when you stop walking around thinking the world owes you, you stop holding others to impossible standards too. You become less reactive. Less resentful. Less disappointed by every unmet expectation.

You give people more grace. More room to be imperfect.

You start showing up in relationships without keeping score. You give more freely, your time, your kindness, your energy, not because it is owed in return but because that's who you are. That's the life you are building.

Not one where you wait for what is yours. But one where you create what matters. That is the power of letting go of entitlement. It does not make you passive. It makes you free. It puts your energy where it actually belongs. In your choices, your actions, your character.

Because here's the secret: the world may not owe you anything, but you still have so much to offer it.

So offer it. Offer your effort. Offer your care. Offer your ideas. Offer your time. Offer your growth.

Not because you are guaranteed anything in return. But because that is who you have decided to be.

Not a victim of what was not given.

But a builder of what can still be.

That is common sense.

No One Is Thinking about You as Much as You Think They Are

You walk into a room and suddenly you're hyper-aware of everything.

Aware of the way you're standing. Aware of the tone of your voice. Aware of that one thing you said that might have come out wrong. You wonder if people noticed. If they're judging you. If you're coming across the right way.

We've all been there.

Overthinking. Replaying conversations. Questioning our tone, our timing, our expressions. Wondering if we seemed awkward or off or just a little too much.

But here's the truth that can save you a lot of energy: No one's thinking about you as much as you think they are.

They're not obsessing over your outfit. They're not analyzing your phrasing. They're not dissecting that thing you said in the group chat. Most of the time, they're too busy thinking about *themselves*. Their own worries. Their own insecurities. Their own awkward moments.

Just like you.

That's the secret most people never say out loud: everyone's in their own head.

We assume the spotlight is always on us. That every move we make is being watched. That every word we say is being evaluated. That every tiny misstep is being judged, remembered, talked about. It feels like we're walking around on a stage, lights blazing, audience watching, every gesture under scrutiny. So we adjust. We monitor ourselves. We double-check what we said. We rework our tone. We try to manage how we're coming across, all the time.

Mindset and Perspective

But here's the thing: most people aren't paying that much attention.

Not because they don't care. But because they're busy. Caught up in their own heads. Thinking about what *they* just said. What *they* are wearing. How *they* came across. Whether *they* looked nervous. Whether *they* talked too much. Whether *you* liked them.

They're dealing with their own doubts, their own distractions, their own to-do lists and insecurities and overthinking loops. So whatever awkward thing you said? Whatever nervous laugh or clumsy wave or half-baked opinion you shared? It probably didn't even register. And if it did, it was likely forgotten in a matter of minutes.

Because the truth is, everyone's walking around thinking they're in the spotlight.

This realization isn't meant to make you feel invisible. It is meant to set you free.

Because the moment you stop assuming the world is watching your every move, you can finally relax. You stop performing. You stop managing your image in every interaction. You stop carrying the weight of constant self-consciousness.

You just get to be.

Think about how often you walk away from a conversation and immediately start replaying it in your head. You analyze every detail. Every word you said. Every pause. Every facial expression. You wonder if you sounded weird, if you talked too much, if your joke landed, if that one thing you said came off the wrong way. You scan for signs you might've made things awkward. You dissect the tone of your voice, the look on their face, the way they responded. You build an entire narrative around a five-minute exchange.

Now flip it.

How often do you do that for other people?

How often do you walk away from a conversation thinking deeply about their tone, their facial expressions, their wording, their little quirks or stumbles?

Probably not often.

Not because you're cold or uninterested. But because you've got your own mind to deal with. Your own conversations to replay. Your own worries and distractions and mental noise.

Most of the time, once a conversation ends, you move on. You think about your next task, your next interaction, your own unfinished thoughts. You don't sit there examining someone else's every word.

And if you're not doing that to others, what makes you think they're doing it to you?

They are not. At least, not the way you imagine.

They're moving on, just like you do. Which means you're probably being a lot harder on yourself than anyone else ever was.

You move on. You forget. You've got your own life to deal with. And so do they.

Most people are not keeping score the way you think they are. They're not remembering your stumbles or awkward phrasing or the weird thing you said when you were nervous. They're not whispering about you on the ride home or bringing it up days later. If anything, they're thinking about whether *they* came across the right way. Whether *you* liked *them*.

It is a little funny when you think about it. Everyone is worried about how they are perceived by people who are equally worried about how they are perceived.

It is one giant misunderstanding. We think they are focused on us.

Mindset and Perspective

They think we are focused on them.

When you believe the spotlight is always on you, you start to shrink. You play it safe. You water yourself down. You hold back your questions, your opinions, your personality, all in the name of not being too much. You aim to be likable, impressive, and acceptable.

But in the process, you disappear a little.

You trade authenticity for approval. And most of the time, no one even notices the trade. Because they're not watching you like that. They are too busy worrying about their own missteps, their own image, their own flaws. What feels huge to you barely registers for them.

So what if you spoke a little too fast? So what if you fumbled your words or had spinach in your teeth or waved awkwardly across the room? It's not a headline. It is just a moment. A blip in time. And if someone did notice it? They probably forgot about it five minutes later.

You don't have to be perfect. You just have to be real.

And you don't have to manage people's perception of you every second. You're allowed to relax. You're allowed to take up space without constantly editing yourself. You're allowed to say the wrong thing once in a while. People do it all the time.

This does not mean you stop caring about how you show up. It does not mean you go around being careless or rude. It just means you stop assuming that every little misstep is a major event. That everyone noticed. That everyone is still thinking about it.

They are not.

And if they are?

That says more about them than it does about you.

The people who obsess over your mistakes, who magnify your flaws, who retell your missteps like stories are not your people. They are spectators, not supporters. You do not need to keep adjusting yourself for their comfort.

You weren't put on this earth to be perfectly palatable to everyone.

You were made to be yourself, fully, freely, even clumsily sometimes.

And the more you let go of the need to be perceived perfectly, the more peace you'll feel.

Because when you stop centering yourself in every story, you stop assuming every reaction is about you. You start giving people more grace. You stop internalizing things that have nothing to do with you. You realize that someone's silence might be about their stress. Their distance might be about their own day. Their short tone might be about something that happened hours before you ever walked into the room.

Not everything is a reflection of you.

That is the ego's trick. It tries to make you the center of every story. Maturity means stepping back and remembering that other people are living complex, full, messy lives too. Sometimes their energy, their words, and their choices are about them, not you.

That shift in perspective? It's powerful.

Because it gives you room to breathe. Room to stop taking everything so personally. Room to stop rewriting your entire personality based on how someone reacted once. Room to stop spiraling after every interaction.

It also helps you become a better listener. A better friend. A better partner. When you're not so wrapped up in how you're being perceived, you can finally start to *see* other people. You stop looking for signs that you're doing something wrong, and you start looking for ways to connect.

You become less defensive. Less self-conscious. More present.

And that is when things start to shift. Not just in how you feel, but in how others experience you.

People are drawn to those who are relaxed in themselves. Not arrogant. Not loud. Just at ease. Comfortable in their own skin. The kind of person who doesn't need to be the center of attention, but also doesn't disappear. They just show up as they are. And somehow, that gives everyone else permission to do the same.

So let go of the idea that everyone is watching.

They are not.

They are wrapped up in their own lives, their own worries, their own doubts, plans, and problems. You are not the center of their world. Let that be a relief. It means you have more freedom than you think. It means most of your mistakes pass unnoticed.

The things that truly matter, like kindness, steadiness, and honesty, are the ones people remember.

Because once you stop trying to manage everyone's opinion of you, you get to focus on the only opinion that really matters: your own.

Live in a way that *you're* proud of.

Say what you mean. Be kind. Be honest. Be real.

Let people see who you are and let go of the ones who don't get it.

You are not here to impress the whole room.

You are here to be *you*.

That is not arrogance. That is peace.

That is common sense.

You Can't Control Others, Just Your Response

It would be nice if people always did what they said they would. If they were honest, thoughtful, and consistent. If they responded to you with the same care that you give them. If they listened. If they followed through. If they handled things with maturity.

But they don't.

People disappoint.

They pull away when things get hard. They shut down when things get uncomfortable. They say things they don't mean, or don't say what they should. They get defensive. They avoid. They lie, or lash out, or ignore. And no matter how thoughtful or reasonable you try to be, there's one truth that always holds:

You can't control them.

Not their tone. Not their timing. Not their choices, their beliefs, or their behavior. You can hope. You can influence. You can model a better way. But in the end, people are going to do what they're going to do, even when it doesn't make sense to you. Even when it hurts.

And that can feel deeply frustrating. Especially when you're trying. When you're showing up with honesty, with patience, with care. You want to believe that if you do everything right, the other person will respond in kind. You think, *if I stay calm... if I say the right thing... if I'm generous enough, kind enough, clear enough... maybe they'll get it.*

Sometimes they do. But sometimes, they don't.

And that's not a failure on your part.

That's just a reminder: they are not in your control.

Mindset and Perspective

You don't get to edit someone's emotional responses.

You can be calm. You can be kind. You can choose careful words with a good heart. People will still respond through their own filters, history, and mood. You may think you are being reasonable, but they may not receive it that way. You do not control their inner reaction.

You don't get to make them see what they refuse to see.

You can try. You can explain with patience. You can be as clear and grounded as possible. But if they are not ready, if they are stuck in denial or defensiveness, nothing you say will land. They will twist your words. They will shut you out. And you will be left wondering what more you could have done, when the answer is nothing.

You don't get to force their growth.

You cannot make someone understand just because you need them to. You might see the pattern clearly. You might be rooting for their breakthrough. But change does not happen on demand. It happens in its own time. Their time.

And sometimes, it never happens.

That's the hard part. Watching someone stay stuck. Knowing they could do better. Knowing the dynamic could shift. If they just saw it. If they just admitted it. If they just took one small step toward it. The whole story could be different. But they don't. Or they won't.

But you're not powerless.

You still get to choose how you respond.

That's where your power lives. Not in trying to change other people, but in learning how to steady yourself regardless of what they do. Your strength isn't found in getting them to behave differently. It is in staying grounded even when they don't. It is in staying calm when the moment tries to shake you. It is in holding your center, no matter how off balance the other person becomes.

You can't control their reaction, but you can control your tone. You can choose to respond, not react. You can speak with calm even when they speak with heat. You can show up with clarity even when they show up with confusion. You get to decide what energy you bring into the room.

You can't control their mindset, but you can decide whether or not to engage. Whether or not to let the conversation continue. Whether or not to protect your peace or pour it out for someone who's not listening. That choice, to step in or step away, is always yours.

You don't have to join their storm.

You don't have to rise to their chaos or match their energy. You can stay grounded. You can stay steady. You can stay rooted in your own peace, even when everything around you tries to pull you out of it.

And that's where real power lives: not in what you control outside of you, but what you master within.

Sometimes that means speaking up, calmly, directly, with clarity. Sometimes it means saying nothing and walking away. Sometimes it means drawing a line. Not to punish, but to protect. Not to change them, but to maintain your peace.

Because you can have boundaries without bitterness.

You don't need to be cold to be clear. You can say no without being harsh. Boundaries aren't about pushing people away. They are about protecting what matters. You can draw the line without raising your voice.

You can be kind without being passive. Kindness isn't silence. It is not self-abandonment. You can be thoughtful and still speak up. You can care about others and still stand your ground.

You can be clear without being cruel.

Mindset and Perspective

Truth does not have to come with sharp edges. You can be honest without tearing someone down. You can deliver clarity in a way that still respects the relationship and yourself.

And when you stop tying your peace to someone else's behavior, you get your power back.

You stop reacting to their chaos. You stop shrinking yourself just to keep things smooth. You stop letting their moods pull you up and down like a string. You remember that their storms are not your storms, and you do not have to carry them. Slowly, your peace returns to you. It is yours again. Steady. Solid. Unshaken.

It is easy to think that if someone would just change, then you could feel better. If they just apologized. If they just understood. If they just stopped doing that thing that gets under your skin. But that puts your emotional well-being in someone else's hands. Someone who might not have the tools, the awareness, or the willingness to hold it well.

That's not stability. That's emotional outsourcing. And it rarely ends well.

You can care deeply about someone and still accept that you can't control their behavior. You can love someone without making their growth your responsibility. You can hold space, offer support, and extend grace, but you can't do their work for them. You can't carry their half of the relationship. And you can't fix a dynamic that takes two to heal.

What you can do is decide who you want to be in the face of it.

You can choose to respond in a way that aligns with your values. You can hold your ground without raising your voice. You can pause when everything in you wants to react. You can let their energy stop with them, not spill into you.

That's emotional maturity. Not reacting just to prove you're right. Not matching their tone just because it feels justified. Not taking their behavior as a mirror for your own.

You don't have to be a reflection. You can be an anchor.

It is not easy. Some people will push your buttons. Some will trigger every instinct to explain, to defend, to correct. But every time you respond with clarity instead of chaos, you're reclaiming your peace. You're saying, *I won't be pulled into your storm. I'll stay in my calm.*

That does not make you passive. It makes you powerful.

It means you're not letting someone else's worst moment define your own. It means you don't need them to be different in order for you to feel okay. It means you've separated who you are from how someone else behaves. And that's one of the healthiest things you can do.

You won't always get it right.

You'll have moments where you lose your cool, where you say the thing you wish you hadn't, where you react instead of respond. That's human. But the more you practice self-awareness, the quicker you recover. The more you notice your patterns, the less power they hold.

And every time you come back to yourself, you're getting stronger.

So no, you can't control them.

But you can control yourself.

And that is enough.

More than enough.

That is common sense.

Discipline Beats Motivation

Motivation is great. When it shows up.

It gives you energy. It makes everything feel possible. It lights a fire under you and gets you moving. You feel focused and ready. Today is the day you will finally turn the corner.

You start visualizing the best version of yourself. You see yourself waking up early, making healthy choices, getting through your to-do list, finally writing the book, starting the business, cleaning the house, running the miles.

You feel sharp. Ready. In control. You are motivated, and suddenly, things that used to feel hard don't seem so hard anymore. You've got momentum, and that momentum is energizing.

You start telling yourself: *this time will be different.*

You make the plan. You organize the schedule. You write the list in clean bullet points. You might even buy new supplies. New shoes. A new notebook. A new app to track your progress. It all feels so fresh, so full of promise. For a moment, you're convinced that nothing can stop you.

And to be fair, that kind of energy can be powerful. It can help you begin. It can help you break out of a rut. It can remind you what you're capable of when you're clear and committed. But as good as it feels in the moment, it's still temporary.

Motivation gets you started. Discipline keeps you moving.

But here's the problem: motivation is unreliable.

Motivation comes and goes like the weather. Some days, it's there before you even open your eyes. Other days, it's nowhere to be found. It is moody. It is fleeting. It depends on your mood, your environment, your energy level, your sleep, your stress, things that shift all the time.

And if you build your life around waiting for motivation, you'll spend most of your time waiting.

This is where discipline comes in.

Discipline is different. Discipline is not loud or flashy. Discipline is quiet. It does not give you a rush. It does not care whether you feel like it. It just says: *we do this anyway.*

Discipline does not need a pep talk. It does not ask how you feel. It does not check for inspiration. It shows up on time, rolls up its sleeves, and gets to work.

Discipline is what carries you when motivation flakes.

It is what gets you to the gym when you'd rather scroll your phone. It is what helps you finish the boring parts of a project. It is what gets the dishes done, the workout finished, the deadline met, even when you're tired or distracted or over it.

Discipline is what creates consistency.

And consistency is what creates results.

It is easy to be motivated for a week. Anyone can show up strong for a few days when the energy is high. When the goal is fresh in your mind, when your playlist is pumping, when your planner is still clean and color-coded, it feels good to be in motion. You feel proud. Productive. Like you're finally doing the thing you've been meaning to do for months. And in those early days, it doesn't take much to keep going. You're fueled by the newness. The excitement. The hope.

But then reality shows up.

You get tired. The schedule gets messy. Life throws you a few curveballs. Maybe the progress isn't as fast as you hoped. Maybe

Mindset and Perspective

you're sore, or discouraged, or distracted. The early wins stop coming. The novelty wears off. And now the thing that felt exciting starts to feel ordinary. Inconvenient. Maybe even a little annoying.

This is the part where most people quit. Not because they don't care. Not because they're weak. But because they were relying on motivation to carry them, and motivation never sticks around for the whole journey.

Because discipline isn't about pushing harder. It is about deciding once.

It is about removing the daily debate from your mind. You don't wake up and ask yourself, "Do I feel like it today?" You already answered that question. You made the choice when you built the habit. Now it's just part of your day, like brushing your teeth or locking the front door.

You might not always enjoy it. But you trust it.

And that's the difference.

Motivation is emotional. Discipline is structural.

Motivation says: do it when you feel inspired.

Discipline says: do it because you said you would.

Motivation is a spark. Discipline is a system.

If motivation is the fuel, discipline is the engine. The spark may get you started, but the engine is what keeps you going. Fuel on its own just sits there. It only becomes useful when the engine puts it to work.

Discipline is the boring stuff that moves you forward. The part no one sees. The part you don't post. The part that looks like nothing is changing, until one day, everything is. Without discipline, motivation fizzles before it takes you anywhere.

Think about athletes. Artists. Writers. Entrepreneurs. Anyone who's good at what they do. Anyone whose work or craft, or performance you admire. Most of their progress didn't come from magical bursts of motivation. It didn't come from waiting for the perfect mood, the perfect conditions, or the perfect idea. It came from showing up. Especially on the days when they didn't feel like it.

The early mornings when the bed was warm but the gym was cold. The blank pages when the words didn't flow. The long stretches of practice when the results were invisible. The emails that didn't get answered. The work that got ignored. The hours spent refining something no one would ever fully see or appreciate. They kept showing up anyway.

When it wasn't fun.

When it was inconvenient.

When it felt repetitive and thankless.

When the applause wasn't there and the progress was hard to measure.

They didn't keep going because they were driven by constant inspiration. They kept going because they made a decision: *this matters, so I'll do it anyway*. Even when it was hard. Especially when it was hard. That kind of discipline becomes the engine behind growth.

Here is the surprising part. That is usually when they make the biggest leap.

Not during the highlight moments, but during the quiet ones. When no one was watching. When the work felt flat. When the urge to quit was strong but they didn't give in. That's when something shifted. That's when the muscle got stronger. When the skill sharpened. When the mindset hardened in the best way.

The growth didn't happen because they were inspired.

Mindset and Perspective

It happened because they showed up regardless.

That's how discipline builds momentum. One boring day at a time.

There's a story I once heard about a guy who started going to the gym, but he gave himself a rule: he only allowed himself to stay for five minutes. That's it. Five minutes, then he had to leave. People thought it was ridiculous. But he wasn't trying to get fit overnight. He was trying to become someone who showed up. Once the habit was in place, the minutes added up on their own.

That's discipline.

It is not about punishing yourself. It is not about pushing until you break. It is about building the muscle of showing up. And the only way to build that muscle is to use it. Even when you're not in the mood.

Especially when you're not in the mood.

That's where discipline grows.

There will be days when it's easy. When the motivation shows up. When everything flows. But those aren't the days that shape you. The days that shape you are the ones when your mind says, "Skip it," and your discipline says, "Do it anyway."

And you do it.

Not perfectly. Not enthusiastically. Just consistently.

That's where the wins come from.

Discipline also gives you freedom.

That might sound backwards, but it's true. When you have discipline, you stop relying on willpower. You stop scrambling. You stop making the same decisions over and over again. You stop being at the mercy of your moods. You get your time back. You get your energy back. You gain control over your day instead of letting your day control you.

Discipline Beats Motivation

Discipline is what makes space for inner peace.

Because you're not constantly negotiating with yourself. You are not chasing motivation like it's a butterfly that might land if you are lucky. You've built a system that supports who you want to be. And you live inside that system, one choice at a time.

And sure, some days you'll slip. That's part of it.

But discipline does not mean perfection. It means you come back.

You miss one workout, not six. You break the habit once, not forever. You fall off track, but you know how to return. And the more you practice that, the stronger your discipline becomes. Until one day, the thing that used to be hard becomes automatic.

You don't dread it. You just *do* it.

And people will say, "You're so motivated."

But you'll know the truth.

You're not motivated. You're disciplined.

Discipline is not loud. It is a promise kept in small pieces.

Pick one thing. Do it today. Do it again tomorrow. When it gets boring, keep going. Keep going when it feels slow. Keep going when it feels ordinary. Boring is where progress hides. Boring is where the real change is happening, even if you cannot see it yet. Stay with it. Trust it. Keep going.

Decide once. Show up. Keep your promise. Results stack. Confidence grows.

Life shifts because you kept moving forward.

Not with a mood. With a habit. Not with a spark. With a structure.

That is not magic.

That is common sense.

Confidence Is Quiet, Insecurity Is Loud

You can feel the difference, even if you don't notice it right away. Some people walk in and try to take over the room. They talk too much. They laugh a little too loud. Their stories sound more like performances than conversations. They want to be noticed. Badly. And they do not care how much noise it takes to get it.

But real confidence doesn't need to do all that.

Confidence does not rush to prove itself. It does not need a spotlight or applause to feel valid. It does not try to outshine, outtalk, or outsmart everyone in the room. It just shows up. Calm. Unshaken. Grounded.

Insecurity, on the other hand, is often loud. It fills silence with noise. It overshares. It interrupts. It talks over people. It tries too hard. It wants to be admired, validated, and praised. Not because it's arrogant, but because it's unsure.

That's the thing: the louder the performance, the deeper the fear behind it.

Confidence and insecurity can sometimes look similar at first glance. Both can speak up. Both can take space. Both can be loud, assertive, or charismatic. But surface-level behavior doesn't always tell the full story.

The energy underneath is completely different.

One is grounded. Calm. Sure of itself, even in silence. The other is scrambling. Reaching. Hoping you won't notice how unsure it really feels.

Confidence is like a tree.

It stands still. It doesn't move to prove anything. It doesn't chase attention. It grows quietly, season by season. Its roots go deep, even if no one sees them. You don't need to hear it rustling to know it's strong.

Insecurity is more like a firework.

Flashy. Loud. Impossible to ignore. For a moment. It explodes in the sky, makes a scene, grabs attention. And then it's gone. The light fades. The noise disappears. And all that's left is smoke.

That's the difference.

One is steady. The other burns out fast.

Confidence doesn't need to compete. It is not scanning the room to figure out who's more impressive, who's getting the most laughs, or who's holding the spotlight. It doesn't feel the urge to jump in and outdo someone's story. It doesn't talk just to be heard. It can sit in silence without feeling small. It doesn't need to be the smartest person in the room or win every point in a discussion.

Confidence is secure enough to say less, listen more, and let others shine. Because it knows that someone else being great doesn't make you any less. That's the quiet strength of someone who understands their own worth. Because confidence is not busy proving itself. Confidence leaves room for others to feel seen too.

Insecurity can't do that. It clings to comparison like it's survival. It walks into a room already measuring, trying to figure out how to stack up, how to stand out, how to stay ahead. It interrupts to stay in control of the narrative. It brags, exaggerates, or twists conversations to sound more impressive.

Insecurity tells stories not to connect, but to dominate. It treats every moment like a performance, and every interaction like a competition. Because underneath it all, there's a fear. That if it's not louder, funnier, smarter, or more accomplished than the people around it, then it won't be enough. And that fear drives everything.

Mindset and Perspective

But confident people don't need to be more. They're just comfortable being themselves.

That's what draws people to them.

Confidence is okay with saying, "I don't know." It doesn't see that as weakness. It sees it as honesty. It understands there is strength in admitting you are still learning and still figuring things out. It has no interest in pretending to have all the answers just to look impressive. It is comfortable leaving space for uncertainty.

It is also okay with being quiet sometimes.

Confidence does not need to fill every silence or keep the spotlight on itself. It can sit back, observe, and let others speak without feeling left out. It understands that presence is not about constant performance. It is about showing up with intention.

Confidence asks questions without shame. It listens more than it talks. It does not need to prove that it is the smartest person in the room. It values curiosity over ego. And when it does speak, it is not trying to dominate. It is simply offering something real. It is not about being loud. It is about being grounded. Confidence does not need to impress. It only needs to be itself.

You'll see it most clearly in how people respond to pressure.

Insecure people often become defensive. Even the smallest suggestion can come across as a threat. They react strongly to criticism, no matter how softly it is delivered or how kind the intention behind it may be. Rather than listening to what is actually being said, they immediately shift into protection mode. Their focus moves away from the message and toward maintaining their image.

They deflect blame. They shift the responsibility onto someone else. They look for ways to explain their actions so they do not have to admit fault. In some cases, they dig in deeper and argue their point until the conversation becomes about who is right instead of what needs to be understood. In other moments, they go quiet. They shut down completely, not out of peace, but out of fear.

They do not view feedback as a helpful tool. They do not recognize it as a chance to learn or improve. Instead, they interpret it as a direct hit to their identity. They take it personally. Being wrong does not feel like a simple mistake. It feels like being revealed. It feels like being exposed, as if everyone can see their flaws.

Underneath that reaction is fear. A deep, quiet fear that being imperfect means they will be judged. That every slip will cost them something important. That they will lose connection. That they will no longer be respected or taken seriously.

And so they back away from accountability. Not because they are careless. Not because they want to hurt others. But because admitting a flaw feels too risky, too exposing. In their mind, owning a mistake is not just about the error itself. It is tangled up with their identity. To them, confessing they got it wrong feels like confessing they are not enough.

And that fear is what keeps them stuck.

Because when you're afraid to be wrong, you stop growing. You stop listening. You stop learning. Everything becomes a performance. A defense. A way to protect an image instead of building real strength.

Confidence moves in the opposite direction. It is not afraid to admit a mistake, because it knows a mistake does not define who you are. Confidence is not afraid to listen, because listening does not make you smaller. It makes you wiser.

Confidence doesn't need attention. It doesn't need applause. It doesn't ask for permission or validation. It just is. It shows up quietly, steady and consistent, no matter who is watching.

Not the polished, loud, curated version of confidence you sometimes see online. Not the kind measured in likes or applause.

Mindset and Perspective

But the real stuff. The quiet kind. The kind that feels solid even when no one is watching. The kind built in private, not staged for display.

Confidence grows from showing up when it would be easier to quit. From doing the work when no one else will see it. From proving to yourself, again and again, that you can handle hard things. And each time you do, it settles in a little deeper. Stronger. Calmer. More certain.

And you do not have to fight to earn it. You build it by being honest with yourself, by doing things even when you are afraid, and by learning from the setbacks. Not by pretending you are bulletproof.

The people with the most to prove often speak the loudest. They chase attention, hoping it will fill the gap they feel inside. They talk more, push harder, and try to be seen as important.

But the people who have done the work do not need to say much at all. Their presence speaks for them. You can feel the difference. They are not trying to impress anyone. They are just steady, sure, and real.

So next time you feel the urge to talk over someone, overshare, or outshine: pause.

Ask yourself: *Am I speaking from confidence? Or from fear?*

You don't have to perform to be respected.

You don't have to be loud to be seen.

You just have to be real.

Because confidence is quiet.

That is common sense.

You Don't Need a Reason to Do the Right Thing

We often act like doing the right thing only counts if there's a reward.

We want to know it will pay off. That someone will appreciate it. That it will come back around in our favor. And when it doesn't, when there's no visible benefit, we second-guess whether it was worth the effort.

But the truth is, you don't need a reason to do the right thing.

You don't need to be noticed. You don't need to be thanked. You don't need proof that it mattered. Some actions are worth doing simply because they reflect who you are, not because of what they produce.

Small moments reveal this clearly. The everyday decisions that no one claps for. Holding the door open for someone, even when you're in a rush. Letting a driver merge, even if they cut you off a few minutes earlier. Choosing patience with a customer service rep, even though you're frustrated. Telling the truth when a small lie would save face or get you out of trouble. None of these things are dramatic. They won't make headlines. They won't change the world.

But they shape something important: you.

Most of the time, these choices don't come with rewards. No one gives you a trophy for staying calm. No one celebrates the moment you quietly do the right thing. But they still matter. They build something real inside you. They reinforce the kind of person you want to be. They stack up, one by one, until eventually they become your default. Not because you had to. Not because anyone was watching.

But because you chose to live and act with integrity. Because what you do shapes who you are becoming.

We've been trained to measure everything. To calculate value based on outcome. We want to know the return. *Will this help me? Will it move me forward? Will it make me look good? Will I get credit, or recognition, or some kind of edge?*

It is like we're carrying around an invisible scale, weighing every action against what it might give us. If the benefit is clear, we move. If it's not, we hesitate.

But not everything that matters can be measured.

Some things don't show up on charts or checklists. You can't quantify what it means to treat someone with kindness when they're having a bad day. You can't track the exact impact of choosing honesty over convenience. You can't always see the ripple effect of doing the right thing when it would have been easier not to.

It is like planting seeds you may never see bloom.

But you plant them anyway. Because the act itself matters. Because it says something about who you are. Because a life built only on visible returns is a shallow one. What truly gives life weight is character, trust, and self-respect. Those are not things you can measure. But you plant those seeds anyway.

Kindness. Integrity. Responsibility. These are not transactions. They're not favors you trade for something in return. You don't hand them out only when you think it will benefit you. You live them. You carry them. You return to them because they are principles you live by. They are the foundation you stand on, not a currency to spend. And they are not negotiable.

And their value isn't found in what you get back. It is not about praise, rewards, or being seen as a "good person."

The real value is in what they shape in you. In who you become when you choose them over and over. Especially when it's hard. Every time you act from that place, you reinforce something within yourself. You grow stronger. Clearer. More anchored in your values. And that's something no one can take away from you.

You do the right thing because it's the right thing. That's it.

And when you start to see it that way, something shifts. You stop waiting for the perfect conditions. You stop telling yourself that you will do the right thing when others do. You stop needing people to earn your patience, your kindness, or your respect. You no longer base your behavior on whether someone else is acting the way you think they should.

You stop keeping score.

You stop tracking what you gave and what you got. You stop measuring your effort against someone else's response. You stop expecting others to notice or reciprocate.

Instead, you begin to act from a place of strength. A place that is not focused on results, but on integrity. You do what feels right because it aligns with your values. Because it reflects who you want to be. And that becomes reason enough.

You take responsibility for your part. Your energy. Your choices.

That's where your real strength is.

It is easy to be kind when it benefits you. It is easy to show patience when you're in a good mood. It is easy to tell the truth when it costs nothing. But what about when it doesn't go your way?

What about when it's hard? When it goes unnoticed? When it makes you vulnerable?

That's when it counts most.

Because it's in the hard moments that character is revealed. Not in the polished ones. Not when it's easy. But when it's quiet, uncomfortable, or inconvenient.

When you do the right thing in those moments, you're not just reacting, you're choosing. You're stepping into integrity. And that stays with you, long after the moment passes.

You don't need to be perfect.

But you do need to be consistent.

And consistency means showing up the same way, regardless of who's watching. It means not adjusting your values based on the mood in the room. It means staying steady even when someone else is being rude, thoughtless, or unfair.

Because who you are shouldn't depend on how someone else is acting.

Doing the right thing doesn't mean you never speak up. It doesn't mean you let people walk on you. It doesn't mean being passive. It means holding your ground with respect. It means being kind without being weak. It means being honest without being cruel.

You can stand your ground and still be a good person.

You can set boundaries and still choose patience. You can disagree and still choose respect. You can protect your peace and still treat people well. These things are not opposites. They're signs of someone who knows how to lead themselves well.

And leadership starts with self-respect.

It is tempting to mirror bad behavior. To match someone's tone. To give them what they "deserve." But that just pulls you into their energy. You lose sight of who you are. You let them decide the kind of person you'll be.

That's not power. That's reaction.

Real power is the ability to choose your response, even when you don't feel like it. Real power is when your values are stronger than your emotions.

That's why doing the right thing matters. Especially when it's hard.

Because that's when most people don't.

That's when people give in, lash out, shut down, or justify actions they wouldn't be proud of in hindsight. But if you can hold the line when it's hardest to hold, you'll walk away knowing you stayed true to yourself.

And that kind of peace is worth more than any reward.

You might not get credit. You might not be thanked. But that doesn't make the moment meaningless. You'll still carry the confidence of knowing you handled it well. That you didn't lower yourself. That you chose strength over ego.

You chose alignment over approval.

And that choice adds up.

You don't always see the payoff right away. But every time you choose patience when it would be easier to snap, you're building something. Every time you take responsibility, even when others don't, you're choosing who you want to be. Every time you act with character, especially when no one else is, you're doing the right thing. Not for applause, but because it matters to you.

Doing the right thing might not be loud or impressive. But it's the quiet kind of strength that holds up when everything else starts to fall apart.

So no, you don't need a reason to do the right thing.

You just need to decide that it matters.

Even when the payoff isn't out there.

That is common sense.

Don't Make Permanent Decisions Based on Temporary Emotions

It can happen in a breath. You feel steady, then a comment lands, and your chest tightens. Anger, hurt, fear, frustration. Sometimes all at once. Your world shrinks to the problem in front of you.

In that rush, you look for a big lever. Quit. End it. Block the number. Hit send on the message you will regret. Make the post that will follow you. It feels powerful right now. It can also leave a mark you cannot erase.

Here is the rule for this chapter: Permanent decisions do not care how you felt when you made them. Feelings pass. Consequences stay. When the choice will still matter next month or next year, wait. Breathe. Sleep on it. Decide when your head is clear.

Because emotions, as real as they feel, are often temporary. They move through us like storms, intense, loud, sometimes blinding, but they pass. Decisions, on the other hand, often stay. You can walk away from a job, a relationship, a commitment in a single moment of anger. You can send the message, speak the words, shut the door. But once it's done, it's done. And if you've ever had to clean up the damage from a reaction you later regretted, you know how hard that can be.

That's why learning to pause is so important.

Not to suppress your emotions or pretend they don't matter, but to give them space to settle before you hand them the wheel. You don't need to act in the middle of the storm. You don't need to react while your heart is racing and your mind is spinning. You are allowed to wait. You are allowed to take a beat, to sleep on it, to step away until your thoughts catch up to your feelings.

Because when you act in a peak emotional state, you're not

thinking clearly. That's not a flaw. It is biology.

Your body is in protection mode. Your brain is flooding with chemicals that prepare you to fight or flee, not to weigh pros and cons. So what feels urgent and obvious in that moment might look completely different tomorrow. That's not indecision. That's perspective.

Anger might tell you to burn the bridge. Shame might tell you to disappear. Fear might tell you to run.

But none of those feelings are facts.

They are signals, not instructions. Emotions point things out, but they do not get to steer the ship. They rise up, get your attention. Sometimes they are right. Sometimes they highlight something that needs to change. Sometimes they call you to speak up, or slow down, or take a deeper look at what is going on.

But sometimes they are just echoes. Echoes of fear, of habit, or of old stories you have already outgrown. The shift comes when you realize this.

That is the turning point. Learning to hear your emotions without giving them control. Letting them speak, but not letting them steer. Feeling everything, but still choosing what comes next. Not reacting just because something loud is happening inside you.

That is where real maturity lives. In the space between what you feel and what you choose to do with it.

When you act without pausing, it can feel like strength. It feels decisive, bold, powerful. But sometimes, it's not strength. It is a reaction you haven't sat with long enough.

Real strength often looks like waiting. Like breathing instead of reacting. Like holding back when your whole body wants to jump in and prove a point.

It is the quiet courage to stay still when everything inside you feels

Mindset and Perspective

charged. It is choosing not to match someone's intensity just because they're loud, emotional, or demanding a response.

It is saying, "I'm not ready to respond to this yet," and meaning it. It is giving yourself permission to step away, to take a moment, to cool off before you speak. Not because you're avoiding the issue, but because you care about handling it with clarity, not heat. Strength is not about always having the last word. Sometimes it's about knowing when to wait for the right one.

We rarely make our best decisions when we're flooded with emotion.

Think back to the times you let something slip out in a heated conversation. Or the text you sent too fast. Or the job you walked away from without a plan. At the time, it might have felt right. It might have felt necessary. But later, with a clearer head, it probably felt different.

That shift is your clarity returning. And it's often what we wish had shown up sooner.

This isn't about shutting your feelings down. It is about giving them space to settle before you let them steer. You don't need to act while your heart is pounding and your mind is spinning. You are allowed to wait. Take a beat. Sleep on it. Step away until your thoughts catch up to your feelings.

This isn't about avoiding hard choices. Sometimes walking away is the right thing. Sometimes standing up for yourself is necessary. Sometimes quitting is exactly what you need. But those decisions should come from a place of calm, not chaos. From intention, not impulse. From choice, not pressure.

There's a difference between responding and reacting.

Reacting is instant. It is quick, automatic, and driven by whatever emotion is the loudest in the moment. It often happens before you have had time to think clearly. You say something sharp, you fire

Don't Make Permanent Decisions Based on Temporary Emotions

off the message, you shut down or storm out. It feels urgent. It feels necessary. But it usually comes from a place of emotional overflow, not clarity.

Responding is something else. It is slower and more intentional. It gives you a chance to pause and think. It creates space to ask better questions and see the bigger picture. It lets you bring in not just how you feel right now, but what you know to be true when you are calm. When you respond instead of react, you are engaging with a better version of yourself. The version that includes your values, your long-term thinking, and your ability to see beyond the moment.

That is a mark of emotional maturity: feeling something deeply without needing to act right away. It is not about being emotionless. It is about being anchored. It is knowing that what feels true in a surge of emotion may not hold up an hour later, and trusting yourself enough to wait and see.

This kind of emotional control is not about suppression. It is not bottling things up. It is not being passive. It is actually a form of self-respect. You respect your own future enough to not sabotage it in a temporary storm. You protect your values, your relationships, and your peace by choosing when and how to act.

The people who navigate conflict well often aren't the ones who never feel angry or overwhelmed. They're the ones who've learned to let the emotion pass before they speak. They take their time. They cool off. They remember what actually matters before making decisions they can't undo.

Letting emotions pass does not mean ignoring them.

It means acknowledging them without handing them control. It means saying, "I see you, but you don't get to decide." It means sitting in the discomfort without needing to escape it through quick, reactive behavior.

And over time, you realize that most situations don't actually need an immediate response. Most things can wait. And most of the things that truly matter benefit from space and thought.

Even five minutes can change how you see a situation. Even one night of rest. Even one honest conversation with someone who isn't caught in the same storm. These small pauses give you the clarity that intense emotion tries to steal. And when you act from that place, the calm after the storm, your choices feel better. They hold up over time.

That doesn't mean you'll always get it right. You'll still have moments where something slips out too fast, or you hit send too soon. But the more you practice, the more you learn to recognize the feeling: that tight urgency that says, *Do something now*.

That is your cue.

Not to act. But to pause.

Because permanent decisions don't care how you felt when you made them. They don't reverse just because the feeling passed. They stay.

So let the feeling pass first and then decide.

You don't have to solve the emotion in order to wait. You just have to not let it lead. That alone can protect you from so many messes, regrets, and apologies you never needed to make.

You are allowed to step back.

You are allowed to say, "Not yet."

You are allowed to wait until your emotions catch up with your wisdom.

That is not weakness.

That is common sense.

Better Late than Never

You may have waited too long. You may have ignored the signs. You may have put it off when it was easier, more convenient, or less uncomfortable to do nothing. You may have missed your best shot. You probably know this already. Some chances do not come around twice. That part stings.

But here is what matters now.

You can still act. Even now. Even if it feels late. Even if it feels awkward. Even if you are carrying more doubt than confidence. You can still make a move. You still have choices. You still have power. You are not out of time, no matter how much time you have already lost. You may not be early, and you may not feel ahead, but you are not finished.

You are not locked in place. You can still begin. You can still take a new path. You can still change direction, even if you have been on the wrong one for a while. You can still turn around. You can still fix something that has been broken for too long. Even if you were the one who broke it. Even if you ignored it. Even if you walked away from it. Repair is still possible. Progress is still possible. A future that looks different from your past is still possible.

Better late than never does not mean everything is fine.

It means it is not too late to make it better than it is now. It means that even if you missed the first door, the second one is still open. And stepping through that second door is better than standing still in front of the first one, wishing you had acted sooner.

You will not always get another chance. That is true. Some windows close and do not open again. Some moments pass and do not return. That is part of life. You will miss things. You will lose time.

But sometimes, you do get another chance. Sometimes the door is still open. Sometimes the opportunity is still there, just waiting for you to stop hesitating. And when that happens, when life gives you one more shot, it's worth taking. Even if it feels small. Even if it feels uncertain. Even if it does not come in the same form it once did.

A second chance is still a chance. And it is worth stepping toward it instead of turning away.

Some things will be harder now. But they are still possible. And often, still worth doing.

You may have missed the years when investing young would have paid off most. But starting now is still better than doing nothing. One dollar put away now is still worth more than zero. One year of compound growth is better than none. One good habit with money today will do more for your future than a hundred regrets about yesterday.

You may have stayed too long in a job you outgrew. Or avoided a career change out of fear or comfort. And maybe the road is steeper now. But it is still your road. And it's still there.

You can still learn a new skill. You can still go back to school. You can still build something that fits who you are now, instead of staying stuck in a version of you that no longer fits.

You may have let a friendship drift. You may have stayed silent when you should have spoken. You may have said something that hurt someone you love. But a late apology is better than no apology. A delayed conversation can still bring healing. Even if it's not perfect. Even if it's hard. Even if you have to carry the awkwardness. You can still make things right.

You may have neglected your health. You may have made excuses for too long. But your body still responds to care. It still benefits from movement, from rest, from nutritious food. The best time to take care of yourself may have been years ago. The next best time is today.

You may have held yourself back from things you wanted to do. You may have told yourself you were not ready. And maybe you were not. But you are more ready now than you will be tomorrow. And every day you wait, you trade progress for comfort. One of those will serve you. The other will keep you stuck.

There is no guarantee that acting now will fix everything.

Starting to save money today will not erase the years you did not. Reaching out to someone you hurt will not undo what happened. Taking care of your health now will not erase all the damage already done.

But not acting guarantees nothing will change.

If you do nothing, the gap stays. The regret stays. The problem keeps growing. Progress does not come from waiting. It comes from doing something, even if it is late, even if it is hard, even if it does not fix everything right away.

Better late than never is not a slogan. It is a mindset. It is the choice to do something real instead of holding onto regret like it is all you have left. Regret will never turn into progress unless you move.

Some people do start early. Some people figure things out quickly and take action before the rest. That is great when it happens. But most people are not like that. Most people are late to something. Late to learning. Late to growing. Late to apologizing. Late to taking their life seriously. And that is not the end of the story.

What matters more than when you start is that you start at all. The timing might not be what you hoped for. You might carry frustration, doubt, or embarrassment about how long it took. But the moment you take that first step, something shifts.

The first step still counts, even if it comes after a long delay. It still moves you. It still matters. It still opens the door to everything that can happen next.

What separates people is not the timing. It is not who started early or who figured it out first. It is the choice to move forward, even after waiting too long. Even after falling behind. Even after thinking it was too late.

You do not have to pretend you are right on schedule.

You do not have to convince yourself that everything happened at the perfect time. You do not need to make excuses or tell a story that makes the delay look intentional. You are allowed to admit that you waited too long. You are allowed to acknowledge that you could have acted sooner. That honesty does not disqualify you. It frees you.

You do not have to lie to yourself about how much time you wasted. You do not have to cover it up or push it aside. You can face it. You can say it out loud. I waited. I hesitated. I ignored it.

And still, even with all of that, you can begin now. You just have to look honestly at where you are, without judgment or denial, and ask yourself some simple questions. *Is staying here worth it? Is staying stuck worth the comfort of avoiding change? Or is it time to move forward, even if it is late?*

It is not about the perfect moment. You may have missed it.

What matters most is the moment in front of you. The real one. The one you actually have. It may be messy. It may be uncertain. But it is yours. And it is enough to begin.

Begin late. Begin uncertain. Begin, even with the regret of waiting too long. But begin.

Because starting now is still better than not starting at all.

Better late than never.

That is common sense.

PART TWO

Everyday Habits

Everyday Habits

The little things matter more than you think. Leaving a few minutes earlier can take the rush out of your day. Going to bed instead of scrolling makes tomorrow easier. Writing things down clears your head. None of it is complicated, but it adds up. Small habits free up energy, lighten your load, and slowly shape a better life. This chapter is about the simple routines that quietly build a better life.

Leave Five Minutes Earlier

Leave five minutes earlier.

That is the idea. It sounds almost too small to matter. Like the kind of advice someone might give when they have nothing better to say. But make no mistake, it can change everything.

Five minutes is not much. It is a sliver of your day. You can spend five minutes staring at your phone, reheating your coffee, or looking for your keys. You can lose five minutes without even realizing it. And that's exactly why it matters.

Because five minutes is the difference between being early and being late. It's the difference between walking in with a calm breath or rushing in with an apology. Between being composed or flustered. Between starting your day with clarity or with chaos.

Many of us operate right at the edge of being late. We convince ourselves we know exactly how long things take. We do the math in our heads and cut it close on purpose. If the drive takes fifteen minutes, we leave with sixteen to spare, thinking we have it all timed just right.

Then we add one more thing.

We answer one more message. We scroll for a few seconds longer or linger in the kitchen without any real reason. It feels like we are using the time well.

But what we are really doing is borrowing time from the version of ourselves who has to rush. The one who ends up paying for it later.

The truth is, we do not account for life. Not real life. Real life is not exact. It is messy.

The car needs gas. Your kid cannot find their shoes. Your dog will

Everyday Habits

not come inside. The line at the coffee shop is longer than usual. There is unexpected traffic. You forgot something upstairs. The elevator is slow. And just like that, your cushion is gone.

Now you are rushing.

Your heart rate goes up. Your thoughts get tight. You start moving faster than your body wants to. You get annoyed. You get clumsy. You forget something important. You drive too fast. You snap at someone who did nothing wrong. And by the time you arrive, you are not really there. You are still catching up to yourself.

And this is not just about appointments or meetings. It is about how you move through the day. It is about how you feel when you show up. It is about creating space for your own sanity.

Because here is what no one talks about. Lateness is not just a scheduling issue. It is a stress issue. And it is a self-respect issue. When you are always late, you are telling yourself you do not need breathing room. That your time is not worth protecting. That you are fine living in reaction mode all the time.

But you are not fine. You are worn out. And it shows.

Leaving five minutes earlier is not about perfection.

It is not about getting everything exactly right or running your life like a machine. It is not about flawless routines or never making mistakes.

It is about giving yourself a buffer. A little space that makes room for the unexpected, so one wrong turn or one small delay does not throw off your whole day.

It is not about becoming a robot.

It is about giving yourself a margin for error. A little room between what you plan and what actually happens. A little space between what you expect and what life throws at you.

It is about a margin for life. The kind of space that absorbs the small, unpredictable things. A delay. A distraction. A moment you did not see coming.

It is about a margin for grace. Grace for yourself. Grace for the people around you. Grace for the morning that did not start the way you wanted it to. Grace for the fact that you are human.

It is about building in a little space to breathe. A little pause between one thing and the next. A small stretch of time that is yours, before the world starts asking things from you.

Five minutes is just enough space to collect yourself. To gather your thoughts. To check in for a moment. To remember what you are doing and why you are doing it. To feel like you are not being pulled in five directions before the day has even started.

To move without panic. Without the tight feeling in your chest. Without checking the clock every thirty seconds. Without rushing through the door while still trying to finish a sentence or zip your coat.

To shift from rushing to moving. From reacting to choosing. From feeling behind to feeling ready. That shift is small on the surface, but it changes the whole tone of how you carry yourself.

To feel in control again. Not of everything. Just of your pace. Just of your presence. Just enough to know you are not at the mercy of the moment.

That breathing room shifts how the whole day feels.

When you have five extra minutes, you walk slower. You think more clearly. You speak with more intention. You are less defensive. Less reactive. You do not feel like the world is in your way. You feel like you are in charge.

And that changes the whole tone of your day.

Think about how many times a week you say something like, "I am

Everyday Habits

running late. I am on my way. I just need a minute. Sorry, I'm behind."

Think about how often those phrases come up, not just once, but again and again. How often they show up in your messages, your phone calls, your rushed explanations as you try to catch up.

Think about how often you feel behind before the day even really starts. Before you have taken a breath. Before your shoes are on. Before your mind is even fully awake, you are already trying to make up for lost time.

What if that feeling disappeared?

What if you started showing up early enough to sit for a second and settle yourself?

What if you had time to review the notes before the meeting? Time to glance through the key points instead of hoping you remember them on the spot. Time to feel calm and clear rather than scattered and rushed.

You could walk in without that anxious energy pulling at your shoulders. No rush to find a seat. No fumbling with your papers or checking your phone as you catch your breath.

You could say hello in a way that feels real. Not as a throwaway or a reflex, but as something grounded. Your voice would be calm. Your thoughts would be with you. You would not feel like you just sprinted through your own morning.

What if your day started with calm instead of catch-up?

Five minutes can do that.

But here is the thing. This will not happen by accident. You will not suddenly find yourself with extra time in the morning. You will not magically start arriving early just because you want to. You have to choose it. You have to plan for it.

You have to tell yourself: *I will leave five minutes earlier than I need to*. And then stick to it. Even when it feels silly. Even when you think you do not need it. Even when everything in you wants to squeeze in one more thing.

That last-minute task can wait. The scroll can wait. The second cup of coffee can wait. But your peace should not have to. It is the one thing that carries into everything else. Protecting it makes the rest of the day lighter, calmer, and more manageable.

Leaving five minutes early is an act of respect. For yourself. For your time. For the people you are meeting. For the person you are becoming. It tells the world that you value presence. That you value calm. That you value being prepared instead of being frantic.

And over time, it creates something bigger. It creates consistency. It creates trust. It builds a track record you can lean on when doubt shows up. It creates a version of you that feels solid, steady, dependable, not just in the eyes of others, but in your own. You start to believe yourself when you make a promise. You start to feel your own strength.

Because when you start your day feeling grounded, it ripples. You carry that calm with you. Into the meeting. Into the classroom. Into the conversation. Into the traffic. Into the coffee shop line. People can feel it, even if they cannot name it. And you can feel it most of all.

You do not need to overhaul your whole routine. You do not need a total life reset.

You just need five minutes. Five minutes of margin. Five minutes of space. Five minutes of breathing room.

It is not much.

But it is enough.

That is common sense.

Go to Bed Earlier

This might be one of the simplest pieces of advice in this book.

Go to bed earlier.

Not because it's trendy. Not because it sounds productive. But because it works. Sleep changes everything.

And yet, we treat it like an afterthought.

We push it back to make room for one more episode, one more scroll, one more task, one more conversation that probably could have waited. We act like rest is the reward you get after everything else is done. But by then, there is nothing left of you. Just a tired, overstimulated, foggy version of yourself trying to function on fumes.

You tell yourself it's fine. That you're used to feeling this way. That you can catch up on the weekend, as if rest is something you can delay and store for later. But deep down, you know the exhaustion is building. You know it's not really working.

But your body keeps score. So does your mind.

When you are constantly underslept, everything feels harder. Your patience wears thin. You become more irritable, more emotionally reactive, and less able to concentrate. Small problems begin to feel overwhelming. Ordinary conversations feel heavier, harder to navigate. Your ability to manage stress slips, and so does the kindness and calm you usually bring to the people around you.

Sleep is not just a break from the day. It is a reset.

Your brain cleans itself while you sleep. Not figuratively. Literally. It clears out waste, processes emotion, strengthens memory, and helps you stay mentally sharp. It also regulates your mood and

Go to Bed Earlier

resets your nervous system so you can handle pressure, think clearly, and respond with more patience. Sleep is not wasted time. It is repair time. It is how your body and mind recover from the day.

And when you cut that short night after night, it begins to show. You feel it in your work. In your focus. In your mood. In your ability to listen. In how engaged you are in conversations. In the presence you bring to relationships. And when you do it daily, it really shows.

Think about how different your day feels after a full night of sleep. You wake up with more energy. Your mind feels clearer. You move through your morning without dragging. The small stuff doesn't bother you as much. You handle challenges more ease. You listen without zoning out. You respond instead of react.

You are not running on empty. You are not reaching for caffeine just to feel awake. You are stronger. More present. You feel like yourself again. Not just getting through the day, but actually being there for it. And people around you can feel that difference too.

You handle challenges better. You listen more easily. You think more clearly. You're just more... you.

And yet, we keep staying up too late. Even when we know we will feel it the next day. Even when we promise ourselves we will do better tomorrow.

Sometimes it's just habit. A pattern that formed slowly and never got questioned. Sometimes it's distraction. A way to avoid the things we do not want to feel or think about. And sometimes it's something quieter. Something that looks like control but is really exhaustion in disguise.

You stay up because the day felt like it belonged to everyone else. Work pulled at you. Responsibilities pressed in. Demands piled up. The noise never stopped. And when the chaos finally settled, you wanted to claim a piece of time for yourself. The night becomes that space. The one stretch of hours that feels untouched. The only time that feels like it is yours alone.

So you take it. Even if it costs you. Even if you know you will pay for it in the morning. Because at least for those extra minutes or hours, you feel like you are choosing something. Even if that choice is slowly wearing you down.

That's understandable. But it's still costing you more than it gives.

Because no matter how much fun the late night is, morning always comes. And the version of you who pays the price is the one trying to focus at work, trying to be patient with your kids, trying to hold a conversation without zoning out. That version of you deserves support too.

And that support starts with sleep.

There is something deeply reassuring about ending the day with care. About not dragging yourself to bed as a last resort, but actually deciding to stop. To slow down. To close the day with intention instead of exhaustion.

It means you are not waiting until your body gives out. You are not collapsing into rest because there is nothing left in you. You are choosing it before you reach that point. You are giving yourself permission to pause, to soften, to recover. Not because you are falling apart, but because you value your well-being enough to protect it.

That's not laziness. That's wisdom.

We spend so much energy trying to improve our mornings. We set alarms with big intentions. We create new routines, hoping they will give us structure and focus. We buy planners, journals, apps, tools that promise to make us more productive, more organized, more in control. We write down goals. We stack habits. We try to win the morning so we can win the day.

We try to fix our mornings without touching the thing that shapes them most. How rested we are when we wake up. We add routines. We stack habits. We chase little tricks. But none of it works if we start the day already tired. A good morning is not about what happens after you open your eyes. It is about the state you bring into that moment.

And yet we rarely look at the night before.

We overlook the hours that decide whether we rise ready or worn out. We forget that how we close the day is how we enter the next. A better morning usually starts the night before. The connection is simple. We just need to notice it.

You cannot build a peaceful life on chronic exhaustion. No matter how strong you are. No matter how good you've gotten at pushing through. At some point, it catches up with you. It shows up in ways you did not expect. In burnout that sneaks in slowly. In short tempers that surprise even you. In foggy thinking that makes the smallest task feel overwhelming.

You start to feel like you are always behind. Like you are barely keeping up with your own life. Everything feels a little heavier. A little harder. And even the things you used to enjoy begin to feel like work. That is what happens when rest becomes optional. When you treat sleep like a luxury instead of a need. Eventually, something gives.

Going to bed earlier will not fix everything. But it helps everything feel more manageable.

It gives you the clarity to respond instead of react. The energy to finish what you start. The patience to be kind when it counts. The resilience to bounce back after a tough day.

And no, it's not always possible to get perfect sleep every night.

Life gets busy. Kids wake up. Deadlines run late. Your mind races when you wish it would slow down. There will be nights when rest is short, interrupted, or hard to find. That is part of being human.

But even small shifts help.

If you can move your bedtime just thirty minutes earlier, it can start to change how you feel. Not every night, but more often than not. A little more sleep can mean a little more patience. A little more clarity. A little more strength to face the day ahead. It does not have to be all or nothing. Small adjustments still matter.

That is not just wellness talk. That is biology.

You are not weak because you need sleep.

You are human.

And being human means you have limits. Your body has signals. Your mind has a breaking point. You are not a machine built to run endlessly. You need rest to recover, to think clearly, to feel like yourself again. This is not a flaw. It is how you are wired.

So give yourself that gift. Give yourself that edge. Turn off the screen before your eyes start to sting. Dim the lights. Lower the noise. Let your thoughts settle instead of racing into the night. Let the day end with care instead of collapse.

You do not need to squeeze one more hour out of the evening. You need to let go. Not because you are giving up, but because you are choosing to protect your energy for what actually matters.

Your body will thank you. Your mind will too.

And so will the people who count on you to be calm, patient, balanced, and clear.

That is common sense.

Say No More Often

Say no more often.

Not to be rude. Not to push people away. Not to shut every door and live in a bubble. Say no more often because your time and energy are not unlimited. They are not a bottomless cup that anyone can keep sipping from. If you keep saying yes to everything, eventually you run dry. And once that happens, everyone suffers. Not just you.

Most people are not great at saying no. They fumble. They hesitate. They try to soften it. They turn it into a maybe. Or they say yes out of habit, and regret it five minutes later. Then they spend hours trying to get out of it, or show up resentful and exhausted.

We say yes for all kinds of reasons. We want to be liked. We want to seem helpful. We do not want to cause conflict. We feel bad turning someone down. We do not want to deal with the awkward silence that sometimes follows a firm no. And in that moment, saying yes feels like the easier path.

But here is the truth. Every yes is a trade. You are giving something away. Your time, your energy, your focus, your presence. And often, you are giving it away for something you did not really want in the first place.

We treat time like it is endless.

Like we can just add one more thing to the schedule, one more task to the day, one more favor to the pile. But time is not endless. You cannot make more of it. Once it's gone, it's gone. When you say yes to something meaningless, you are saying no to something meaningful. And you might not even realize it until it's too late.

Saying no is not about being difficult. It is about being clear.

No is a filter. It helps you separate what matters from what does not. It helps you keep your life from filling up with things that leave you drained, scattered, and overstretched.

Think of your attention like a garden. You only have so much water, so much sunlight, so much space. If you say yes to every request, every obligation, every invite, it's like planting too many seeds in too little soil. Nothing grows well. The roots compete. The flowers wither. The whole thing becomes crowded and chaotic. But when you protect that space, when you choose what you plant, the things that matter have room to grow.

Saying no is an act of care.

It tells your future self, *I've got you. I am not going to overload your plate. I am not going to agree to something just because I felt guilty or pressured. I am not going to say yes now and leave you to clean up the mess later.*

You do not have to be cruel. You do not have to be loud. You just have to be honest. A soft no is still a no. A kind no is still a no. It is not about volume. It is about clarity.

But clarity takes practice.

You start by noticing where your automatic yeses come from. Is it fear? Is it guilt? Is it the feeling that your value comes from being agreeable or always available? Pay attention to that moment right before you respond. That little voice that says, *I do not want to do this.* That quiet discomfort you brush aside.

That moment matters. That is the moment to pause.

You do not need a speech. You do not need a long list of excuses. You do not owe anyone a full explanation. A simple, respectful no is enough.

No, I can't commit to that right now. My schedule is already full, and I know I would not be able to give it the time or attention it deserves.

Thanks for asking, but I'm not available. I appreciate you thinking of me, but I have to pass this time.

I'm not taking anything new on at the moment. I'm trying to stay focused on what's already on my plate, and I know adding more would stretch me too thin.

That's not something I can say yes to. It just doesn't align with where I need to focus my time and energy right now.

It doesn't need to be dramatic. It just needs to be true.

And yes, it might be uncomfortable at first. Especially if you are used to being the person who always says yes. Especially if people have come to expect that from you.

You might feel selfish. You might feel rude. You might feel like you are letting people down.

But what you are actually doing is drawing a line. You are setting a clear and healthy boundary. You are saying, *this is where I stop, and this is what I can handle.* You are protecting your limits, not as a way to shut people out, but as a way to stay steady and present in the things that matter most.

You are making sure that when you say yes, you mean it. That it's not something you are saying out of pressure, guilt, or habit. That your yes comes from a place of truth. Fully, honestly, with your whole heart behind it.

There is nothing generous about saying yes when you are burned out. There is nothing noble about overextending yourself to the point where you start resenting the very people you wanted to help. That is not kindness. That is neglecting yourself in the name of pleasing others.

You cannot pour from an empty cup.

When you are drained, exhausted, or stretched too thin, there is nothing left to offer anyone else. You may try, but what comes out will be forced, shallow, or incomplete. You cannot give your attention, your care, or your focus when you are running on fumes.

You cannot give your best when you are running on empty. Not to your work. Not to your relationships. Not even to yourself. When you are depleted, everything suffers. Your patience wears thin. Your thoughts become scattered. Your presence fades, even when you are physically there.

Saying no more often is how you make sure you still have something left to give. It is how you protect your ability to show up fully. It is how you preserve your energy for the things that matter most. It is not a rejection of others. It is a commitment to showing up well when it really counts.

But here's the freeing part. The more you practice saying no, the easier it gets. The less guilt you carry. The more trust you build with yourself. You start to feel the difference between a yes that feels right and a yes that feels forced. You begin to choose with intention, not impulse.

People will adjust.

Some may not like it at first. That is okay. You are not here to be everything to everyone. You are not here to be on call for every favor, every plan, every need that comes your way. You are allowed to say no simply because you do not have the time, or the energy, or the interest.

You are allowed to say no without being defensive. You are allowed to say no and still be a kind person. You are allowed to say no and walk away with peace instead of guilt.

No creates space. Space for rest. Space for focus. Space for the things that actually align with who you are and where you want to go.

You cannot live a meaningful life if you say yes to everything.

The people who respect your boundaries will remain close. They will understand that limits are part of healthy connection. They will not see your no as rejection, but as honesty. They will value the reliability that comes from someone who knows where they stand.

The ones who only stuck around because you were convenient or compliant will drift. Let them. You are not here to carry every load. You are not here to solve every problem. You are not here to meet every need. That is not selfish. That is wise. It is how you keep your strength for what truly matters. It is how you build relationships that last.

And the irony is, when you say no more often, your yes starts to matter more. It becomes clearer. Stronger. More generous. Because it comes from a place of choice, not pressure.

Saying no is not rejection. It is redirection. It is you choosing where your energy goes. It is you saying, *I value my time too much to give it away mindlessly. I respect myself enough to protect my peace.*

It might take time to get comfortable with that. You might slip back into old habits. That is normal. But keep practicing. Keep choosing what matters. Keep noticing how much lighter you feel when you stop saying yes just to avoid a moment of awkwardness.

You are not here to be everyone's backup plan. You are not here to be everyone's automatic yes.

You are here to live your life. And that life deserves space.

So say no more often.

Not with anger. Not with pride.

But with clarity. With respect. With peace.

You are allowed.

That is common sense.

Don't Argue with People Looking for a Fight

Some people are not looking for a conversation. They are looking for a reaction.

They do not want to understand. They want to win. They want to pull you in, get you riled up, wear you down, and then point at your frustration like proof that they were right all along.

And if you are not paying attention, you will fall for it.

You will feel the urge to explain, to defend yourself, to clear the air. You will think that if you just say it the right way, they will finally get it. If you just stay calm and reasonable, they will come around. If you give them facts, they will stop twisting your words.

But people who are looking for a fight are not interested in clarity.

They are not hoping for common ground. They are not trying to see things from your perspective or find common ground. They are not curious about what you think or why you think it.

They are not listening to understand. They are listening to reply. They are waiting for their turn to speak. Waiting for a moment to interrupt. Waiting for you to slip up so they can pounce on your words.

They are listening to catch you. To twist what you said. To throw it back at you in a way that makes you stumble. They want to throw you off balance. They want to make you doubt yourself. They want to make you feel small. Overwhelmed. Cornered. They want to leave you doubting, even when you know you are making sense.

These people do not want resolution. They do not want mutual respect or closure or progress. They want reaction. That is their goal: to get under your skin, to make you flare up, to pull you into a mess you never asked for.

That's why the strongest move is not to out-argue them. It is to refuse to play their game.

Not because you are avoiding conflict, but because you know when a conversation has no real chance of going anywhere useful. You know when someone is not arguing in good faith. You know when your time and energy would be better spent elsewhere.

It takes discipline to stay out of a fight when someone is trying to pull you in. It takes confidence to walk away without needing to prove a point. But that is exactly what wisdom looks like. Knowing what deserves your voice and what does not.

Think about the times you walked away from an argument feeling empty. Your energy drained. Your mind scattered. Your chest still tight from holding so much tension. Frustrated, not because you were wrong, but because you lost your balance. You let yourself get pulled in. You let it run further than it ever needed to.

Not because you were outmatched. Not because your points were weak. But because the whole thing was a trap. A waste. Like stepping into quicksand, thinking it was solid ground. The more you struggled to make your point, the deeper it pulled you in.

By the end, you were not even sure what you were arguing about, only that it had taken something from you.

Something real. Your calm. Your clarity. Your time.

And none of it was worth it.

That is the cost of engaging with someone who is not interested in connection or understanding. You lose peace. You lose focus. You get pulled into a mental loop that plays long after the conversation ends.

You do not owe anyone your presence in that space.

You do not have to show up to every argument you are invited to. You are allowed to let people talk without joining them. You are allowed to say, *This is not worth my energy*, and leave it at that.

Some people use arguments like bait. They toss out a comment, a dig, a loaded question. And when you respond, they pull you in deeper. The only way to win is to not grab the rope in the first place.

It is like a game of tug-of-war. If you hold on, they will keep pulling. But if you let go, the game ends. They might still be shouting. They might still be trying to provoke you. But without your grip, there is nothing for them to fight against.

Letting go does not mean giving up. It means recognizing the difference between a challenge worth meeting and a trap not worth stepping into.

There is a difference between a real disagreement and someone looking for a fight. You can tell by the tone. By the posture. By the way they twist your words or raise their voice or refuse to let you finish a sentence. That is not a discussion. That is theater.

And you do not have to audition for the role.

Save your energy for people who are curious. Who ask questions. Who can disagree without attacking. Who actually listen. They are out there. And they are worth your time.

But the ones who interrupt, mock, roll their eyes, or talk over you are not showing signs of curiosity. They are not trying to understand where you are coming from. They are not interested in hearing you out or building a thoughtful exchange. Their goal is not truth.

They want to stir something up. They want to push your buttons just enough to get a rise out of you. They want conflict, not conversation. They are not listening so they can learn. They are listening so they can argue. They are looking for tension.

Do not feed it.

You will be misunderstood in life. You will be misquoted, misread, or misrepresented. It happens. But you do not have to chase every misinterpretation trying to fix it. You do not have to explain yourself to people who already decided not to hear you.

Your peace is worth more than being right in someone else's eyes. The calm you carry matters. The steadiness you protect matters. The space in your mind that stays clear matters. All of these are more valuable than convincing someone who doesn't want to be convinced. Being seen as right is never worth losing your peace.

Your clarity matters more than winning a pointless argument.

Some arguments go in circles. No matter what you say, it just leads to more jabs and deflections. There is no end. No progress. No real purpose. Walking away is not losing. It is protecting your peace.

This is not about walking away from every hard conversation.

Some conversations are worth having. Some disagreements matter. Some conflicts are the path to deeper understanding. You will know the difference, not by how hard the conversation is, but by whether the other person wants resolution and not a fight.

Fights tear things down. Conversations build things up.

When someone is only interested in tearing, step back. Not out of fear. Out of strength. Out of respect for your time. Out of commitment to your values. You do not have to match their anger with more anger. You do not have to join them in the noise. Stepping back is not weakness. You are choosing to keep your integrity intact.

You are not a punching bag for someone else's mood. You are not a stand-in for the real issue they have not dealt with. You are not obligated to match their volume just to be heard.

Silence is power.

If someone wants a fight and you do not give it to them, they lose the control they were reaching for. They wanted a reaction. They wanted to pull you off balance.

But when you stay calm, when you do not flinch, their grip weakens. You are not giving in. You are not giving them the outcome they expected. And that shifts everything.

They can only spar with someone who shows up swinging. Arguments need fuel. They need someone to push back, to raise their voice, to join the chaos. Without that, it falls flat. The fire fizzles. The energy they were trying to feed starts to die out.

You do not have to swing. You do not have to meet them where they are. You can choose stillness instead. You can choose to keep your calm, hold your ground, and walk away with your peace intact.

And when you do, you will notice something. You feel lighter. You feel stronger. You feel grounded, as if you are standing on solid ground again. The weight you were carrying begins to lift. The tension that held you tight starts to loosen.

Because you chose peace over pride. You chose clarity over chaos. You chose to protect what matters instead of proving a point that did not. And that choice leaves you with something far more valuable: a calm you can trust.

Let others throw their punches in the air.

Let them argue with themselves if they want to.

You don't need to join them.

Not every argument deserves your presence.

That is common sense.

Don't Put off What Takes Less than Two Minutes

If it takes less than two minutes, do it now.

This is one of those rules that sounds too simple to matter. It is the kind of advice that almost feels forgettable. It sounds like something you have heard before and brushed off. Something too ordinary to be important.

It sounds too small to make a difference. Too quick to be meaningful. Just a tiny action that feels like it could not possibly shift anything.

But it does make a difference. It creates momentum. It clears space. It builds a habit of action instead of delay. It might seem small in the moment, but the impact shows up again and again.

Over and over again, it works.

You see a dirty glass in the sink. It would take ten seconds to rinse it. Instead, you walk past it. You tell yourself you'll get to it later. Later becomes an hour. An hour becomes a day. Suddenly the sink is full. Now the job is no longer ten seconds. Now it's twenty minutes and a headache.

Think about paying a bill. You see it come in, set it aside, and think you will deal with it tomorrow. Tomorrow turns into next week. By the time you remember, the deadline has passed and now what could have been a quick payment has become a late fee and unnecessary stress.

The same thing happens with clothes. You toss a shirt on the bed, telling yourself you will hang it up later. Then another joins it, and another. Soon the bed is covered. What could have taken ten seconds now turns into a pile that takes twenty minutes to sort and put away.

Everyday Habits

A bill. A form. A quick reply. A shirt that needs hanging. A dish that needs washing. A receipt that needs saving. A bag that needs unpacking. All of it could be done in less time than it takes to scroll through one more post or watch one more video. And yet we delay.

The little things pile up. And when they do, they start to weigh on you.

You do not notice it at first. But the clutter grows. The mental tabs stay open. You keep thinking, I need to get to that. I should do that soon. It stays in the back of your mind like a quiet hum you cannot shut off. Avoiding small tasks only makes them feel heavier. And they always seem to multiply.

One spoon left on the counter becomes five. One unanswered message becomes ten. A shirt left out becomes a messy room. A two-minute delay turns into two hours of cleaning up things you could have handled on the spot.

It is not about the task. Most of the time, the task is so small it hardly matters on its own. It is not about checking a box or reaching some imaginary level of productivity. It is about momentum.

Doing something right away builds movement.

It gets you unstuck. It takes you out of hesitation and into action. One small step turns into another.

You start moving, and movement tends to continue.

It creates flow. The kind of rhythm that makes the rest of your day feel smoother. When you handle something right away, you create space. Not just on your desk or in your home, but in your mind. The task is finished, and you no longer carry it with you. You are not circling back to it in your head. You are free to move on.

It tells your brain something important. It says, *I take care of things. I do not avoid. I do not push off. I do what needs to be done.*

That builds trust with yourself. A quiet, steady trust. The kind that makes you feel more capable, more focused, and more in control.

And when you trust yourself to act, you start to act more. You build the habit of doing. Not thinking about doing. Not planning to do. Just doing.

It becomes a quiet rhythm. See it, do it, move on. No ceremony. No overthinking. No delay.

You don't waste time convincing yourself to do something that takes less time than the conversation you are having about it in your head. You don't spiral into excuses or overthink the timing. You don't turn a simple task into a mental debate.

You just do it. Quickly. Quietly. Without drama. Before your mind has the chance to complicate it. And once it's done, it's gone. Out of your way. Out of your head.

Two minutes is not much. But it breaks the pattern of putting things off. It cuts through procrastination before it gets a grip. Once you put something off, it becomes bigger in your mind. Heavier. More complicated. It grows in size even when it has not changed.

But if you do it right away, it never grows.

This habit becomes a kind of muscle. The more you use it, the easier it gets. You stop negotiating with yourself about every little thing. You stop turning simple tasks into a decision-making process. You just act.

And that keeps your life cleaner. Calmer. Lighter.

This is not about being perfect. It is not about handling everything at once. It is about not letting the small things collect into something that feels overwhelming.

Think of a room. A space you use every day. If you clean as you go, putting things back where they belong, wiping a surface when it gets dirty, tossing out what you no longer need, the room stays neat with very little effort. A few seconds here, a minute there, it all adds up to a space that feels calm and easy to be in.

But if you let one item stay out, a cup on the table, a jacket on the chair, and then another, and then another, it starts to build. Slowly at first, almost without noticing. Then suddenly, you look around and the room feels chaotic. Things are scattered. It is a mess.

And that mess feels heavy. You don't even know where to start. The idea of cleaning it becomes bigger than the cleaning itself. All because a few small things were ignored one at a time.

The same is true for your mind.

If you handle the small things as they show up, your mental space stays clear. You are not constantly carrying little reminders, open loops, or undone errands. You are not falling behind one tiny delay at a time.

Two minutes may seem like nothing. But ten of those tasks avoided in a day add up to twenty minutes. In a week, that is over two hours. In a month, it becomes a pile of things that could have been done with ease but now feel like a burden.

This rule saves you from that pile.

And there is something else. The more you delay, the more you start to associate everyday tasks with resistance. You begin to dread simple things. You feel like you are always behind, always catching up. That creates stress. Not because the tasks are hard, but because they feel endless.

Doing something right away ends that cycle before it begins.

You send the email. You fold the blanket. You put the shoes back. You reply to the message. It's over. Done. Handled. You are free to move on. That is where peace lives, in the space between things that are finished and things that have not yet become a problem.

Of course, not everything can be done in two minutes.

Some things require planning, energy, or deeper focus. That's fine. But most of the daily clutter, both physical and mental, comes from things that could have been taken care of on the spot.

There is no need to wait for the perfect moment to rinse a glass or hang a shirt. You are already standing there. You already noticed it. That is your cue.

Ignore the little voice that says it's not urgent. That's how messes grow. That's how tasks pile up. That's how stress creeps in. It always feels harmless in the moment. Just one dish left in the sink. Just one bill left unopened. Just one email left unanswered.

But those little delays gather weight. They do not stay small. They multiply. They start to fill your space, your schedule, and your mind. What could have been quick and easy becomes something heavy and annoying. The longer you wait, the bigger it feels. And soon the task you brushed aside is no longer about two minutes. It has turned into clutter, tension, and a nagging reminder that you are already behind.

You are not too busy for two minutes. And those two minutes, done again and again, change how your life feels. You become someone who is not behind. Someone who is not overwhelmed by the basics. Someone who moves through the day with less friction.

You are not chasing tasks. You are clearing them as they come.

So the next time you notice something that could be done quickly: do it.

Do it now. Before you start thinking. Before you start debating. Before it becomes another thing to carry.

If it takes less than two minutes, handle it.

That is common sense.

Make Fewer Promises and Keep Them All

It is easy to make a promise. Easy to say yes.

Yes feels generous. It feels brave. It feels like stepping up. But a promise is not just a kind word. It is a thread you tie between yourself and someone else. A thread that pulls if you forget, frays if you ignore it, and snaps if you stretch it too far.

Most of us make more promises than we realize.

You tell a friend you will call tonight. You tell your manager you will send the draft by Thursday. You tell yourself you will be in bed by eleven. These are not just casual words. They are agreements. Trust grows or shrinks based on how you handle them.

And it is not just the big promises that matter. The little ones count too. The ones you make without thinking. The ones you make just to end a conversation or to avoid disappointing someone in the moment.

Sure, I'll take care of it.

I'll be there for sure.

Let's definitely catch up soon.

You mean well when you say it. But if your calendar fills up or your energy dips or you forget entirely, the promise quietly dissolves. Maybe the other person shrugs it off. Maybe they do not. Either way, something is lost.

This chapter is not about saying yes. It is about promising. There is a difference. Yes can be casual. Automatic. A way to move the conversation along. But a promise is something else. A promise is a commitment that asks for your attention. It means you are putting your name on the line. It means someone is counting on you. What you promise. How you promise. How you carry it. And how you handle it when something slips.

Start by knowing what counts as a promise.

"I should" is not a promise.

"I want to" is not a promise.

"I might" is not a promise.

"I will" is a promise.

A real promise is clear. It has shape. It has weight. It tells someone what to expect, when to expect it, and what it will look like when it is done. It leaves no room for guessing. No fog. No maybe. And that is exactly why you should make fewer of them. Not because promises are a burden, but because they are not meant to be tossed around. They are meant to be trusted.

Not because promises are bad. But because they matter.

The more you say yes without thinking, the more likely you are to drop something important. And when that happens, people notice. They start to wonder if your word is reliable. If they can trust you to follow through. And over time, trust is what holds everything together: friendships, families, teams, reputations.

So give your word less often. But when you do, let it mean something.

Be specific. A vague "I'll get to it soon" leaves room for confusion. A clear "I'll send it by Friday morning" gives both you and the other person something to count on.

Write it down. Put it in your calendar. Not because you are forgetful, but because you are human. A written promise is easier to keep than one floating around in your head.

And if something changes and you cannot keep a promise, speak up early. Do not wait until the last minute. Do not go silent. Do not hope they forgot. Say something. Own it. Offer a new plan. Let them know they still matter to you.

That is how you protect trust even when things go off track.

There is a moment after you realize you might break a promise where you get to choose. You can hide. You can make excuses. You can hope it goes unnoticed. Or you can show up honestly and deal with it directly. That one moment says a lot about your character.

The same goes for promises to yourself. They matter too.

You might not say them out loud, but you hear them in your own mind. You make them in the mirror. In the car. While brushing your teeth or lying in bed at night. Promises like:

I am going to start tomorrow.

I am going to eat better.

I am going to finish this project.

I am going to speak up next time.

I am going to stop saying yes when I mean no.

These are promises too. And when you keep breaking them, something shifts. You stop trusting yourself. You stop believing your own goals. You say the words, but deep down, you no longer expect to follow through. You start to feel hollow.

But when you keep a promise to yourself, even a small one, it does something powerful. It rebuilds the connection between what you say and what you do. It reminds you that you are someone who shows up. Someone who follows through. Someone who does what they say they will do.

And that starts to change how you see yourself.

You do not need a grand gesture. Start with one simple commitment.

If you say you will walk ten minutes, walk. If you say no phone before breakfast, leave it in the other room. If you say you will stretch before bed, stretch. If you say you will drink more water today, start now. Keep that one promise. Then build from there.

Each one builds a little more self-respect. A little more clarity. A little more momentum.

And when, not if, you mess up, be honest. Not just with others. With yourself.

Maybe you got tired. Maybe you overcommitted. Maybe you forgot. It happens. But do not pretend it didn't. Acknowledge it. Adjust. Make a new plan. A broken promise is not the end of your credibility. But pretending it didn't happen is.

You do not have to keep every promise perfectly. But you do need to treat them with care.

The goal is not perfection. The goal is integrity.

Integrity means saying what you mean, meaning what you say, and following through even when it is inconvenient. Especially then. It means staying true to your word not just when it is easy, but when it takes extra effort. When it would be simpler to let it slide. When no one is watching. That's the moment where integrity either holds or breaks.

It is easy to be reliable when life is smooth. It means more when things are busy. When you are tired. When you are tempted to walk away. That's when promises reveal their weight, and when you show what you are made of.

If you are someone who keeps showing up, people notice. They stop checking in because they trust that if you said yes, it is handled. They start relying on you not because you are loud, but because you are steady.

And that kind of steadiness is rare.

It makes you a better teammate, a better friend, a better partner. It makes you someone people want in their corner. Not because you always say yes. But because when you do, they know you mean it.

So pause before you say yes.

Ask yourself:

Can I actually do this?

Will I want to do this when the time comes?

What might get in the way?

Will I still say yes if nobody thanks me?

Am I saying this to avoid awkwardness, or because I truly intend to follow through?

If your answer is shaky, do not promise. It is better to disappoint someone briefly than to let them down later. Better to say no clearly than to say yes and vanish.

And if you say yes, really say yes, then mean it.

Put it in writing. Set a reminder. Show up. Follow through. And when it is done, take a quiet moment to notice what that does for your confidence. For your credibility. For your peace of mind.

You do not need to promise more. You need to mean it more.

Fewer promises. Clearer expectations. Stronger follow-through.

That is common sense.

Leave Spaces Better Than You Found Them

Leave spaces better than you found them.

It sounds simple. Almost too simple to matter. But it is one of those rules that changes the feel of daily life when you practice it.

Think about when you rent a cottage. You arrive, excited for a weekend away. You walk into the kitchen and notice the dishes are not all clean. A little coffee stain in a mug. A frying pan with oil still clinging to it. It's not terrible, but it takes the shine off the place. Someone before you decided "good enough" was enough.

Now picture leaving that same cottage. You take the time to wash every dish properly. You sweep the floor. You wipe the counters. You leave it better than you found it. The next guests walk in and smile. They feel cared for, even though they will never know your name.

That is the habit at work.

It is not just about avoiding complaints. It is about adding a little extra care into the system.

And it can show up anywhere.

At work, it might mean leaving the meeting room cleaner than you found it. You erase the whiteboard so the next person is not staring at your leftover notes. You stack the chairs so the room looks ready instead of chaotic. You throw away the empty cups instead of leaving them for someone else.

No one will clap for you. No one will send you a thank-you email. But the next team that walks in will feel the difference. They will sit down to a space that is ready, not one they have to clean before they can even start.

The same is true in smaller details. When you borrow supplies from a colleague, you return them in good condition. You refill the printer tray if you used the last of the paper. You wash out your mug in the break room sink instead of leaving it for whoever comes after.

These are not grand gestures. They are barely noticed most of the time. But the culture of a workplace is built on these small decisions. A place where people leave things better is a place where trust grows. A place where people always leave messes behind is one where resentment quietly builds.

At a hotel, it might mean gathering the towels in one place or emptying the trash before you check out. Small actions that make the space easier for the person who comes after.

Even when traveling, you notice it.

Walk into a bathroom at a rest stop that has been trashed. Paper is scattered on the floor. Water is splashed across the counter. Soap is dripping down the sink. It drags you down immediately. You do what you came to do, but the whole time you feel tense, wishing you did not have to touch anything.

Now walk into one that has been reset. The floor is clear. The counters are wiped. The trash has been emptied. Everything is simple, tidy, and ready. You breathe a little easier without even realizing it. You feel lighter. Someone cared enough to reset the space before you arrived, and you get the benefit.

The same is true in airports, in train stations, in roadside diners. A space that has been cared for changes how you feel in it. It lifts you instead of weighing you down.

Or picture this. You pull into a shopping plaza and notice a cart sitting at the edge of the parking lot. Someone left it there, far from the cart return. You park, do your shopping, and when you finish you do not just leave your cart where it's convenient. You walk it back to where it belongs.

It takes less than a minute. But the lot looks neater for everyone else. The stray cart will not roll into someone's car. The next shopper does not have to wrestle a cart out of the bushes. A tiny act, but it leaves the space better than you found it.

This habit works at home too.

Clear the counter after cooking so you do not walk back to dried sauces and crumbs later. Make the bed before leaving the room so your return at night feels like a welcome instead of a chore. Close the closet door instead of leaving it open, so the room feels complete, not half done.

Each act is small. Seconds, not minutes. But they save your future self from extra work. They prevent the little jobs from stacking into something big. They keep your spaces from whispering, "Clean me, clean me," every time you walk by.

And the best part? When you walk back in, you feel the difference immediately. You are not facing leftovers from yesterday. You are stepping into a room that is ready for today.

So be the one who leaves spaces better. Be the one who leaves the hotel room in better shape. Be the one who leaves a clean table at the restaurant.

And it is not just about spaces. It is about atmosphere too.

You can leave a room tidier than when you entered, but you can also leave it lighter. The energy you bring with you matters just as much as the objects you move around.

You can walk into a conversation that feels tense and, by the time you leave, the people feel calmer. You can bring patience instead of sharpness. You can bring listening instead of interruption. A few steady words, or even a willingness to stay quiet, can reset the tone.

The same is true with family. Gatherings can carry old friction and familiar patterns. But you can choose to leave less tension behind

Everyday Habits

than when you arrived. You can decide not to fan the flame of an argument. You can be the one who softens the edge with humor, or with kindness, or simply by refusing to escalate.

That is another way of leaving a space better than you found it. Not just in the furniture or the dishes, but in how it feels to be there.

Sometimes leaving things better is about wiping a counter. Sometimes it's about softening the mood. Both matter.

It helps to think of it as stewardship. You are not just a user of spaces. You are a caretaker, even if only for a moment. The world is a shared stage, and you leave it ready for the next act.

Most people never notice when you do it. They only notice when you don't. The dirty pan. The abandoned shopping cart. The chair left askew in a café.

It is okay if no one notices. The point is not applause. The point is respect.

And the respect goes in every direction. Respect for others who share the space. Respect for the people who maintain it. Respect for yourself, because you are worth living in a world that feels cared for.

There is a subtle pride that comes with this. You begin to see yourself differently. You are not the person who takes without giving back. You are the person who adds something. Who smooths the edges. Who makes things a little easier for whoever comes next.

It is not about perfection. It is not about living in spotless rooms or walking through life like a janitor. It is about tipping the balance. One small action. One small improvement.

That's all it takes.

And it is contagious.

When people see you resetting the table, folding the blanket, or pushing in the chair, it nudges them to do the same. The habit spreads without a word.

Imagine if more people lived this way. If everyone returned their cart. If everyone left the borrowed cottage sparkling. It would show respect for the people who come after you. The world would feel a little more cared for.

This is not a complicated philosophy. It is simple. You walk in. You use the space. And before you walk out, you leave it better.

Not perfect. Just better.

That is common sense.

Write It Down: Memory Is Unreliable

Your memory is not as sharp as you think.

It is not a camera. It does not capture every moment with perfect clarity. It does not preserve the exact picture the way it looked or sounded when it happened. It is not a storage drive. It does not file away information in neat folders that stay untouched until you need them again. It is not a clean, well-organized shelf where every detail is placed in perfect order, labeled and ready to be retrieved at any time.

Memory is flexible.

It shifts over time. It changes shape depending on how often you revisit it. It is slippery. Things slide out of reach when you least expect it. A name, a date, a small task you swore you would not forget. It is unpredictable. You never quite know what it will hold on to and what it will let go.

Sometimes it works. Sometimes it pulls something back with surprising clarity. A sound, a face, a phrase someone said years ago. Other times it fails. You search for something you were sure you knew, and it's simply gone. Sometimes it gives you a clear picture of something that never actually happened. A mix of details and assumptions, stitched together like a memory. Other times, it forgets something important within minutes. A thought, a plan, a promise, lost without warning.

That is not a flaw. That is how human memory works. But knowing that means you need to adjust how you operate.

If it matters, write it down.

Do not trust yourself to remember what time the meeting is. Do not trust yourself to remember the idea you had in the shower. Do not tell yourself you will respond to that message later and assume it will stay on your mind.

It won't.

Or it might, but not at the right time.

You will remember the message when you are falling asleep. You will remember the idea when you are already doing something else. You will remember the appointment five minutes after it started.

And the worst part is that it will feel like a surprise. Even though you knew it earlier, it will feel like it vanished out of nowhere.

Because it did.

That's how memory works. It drops things without notice. It lets go of details you were sure would stick. It reshuffles the mental deck when you are not looking, moving yesterday's thought beneath today's distractions. It holds on to the wrong things. The comment you wish you could forget. The worry you never meant to carry.

At the same time, it lets go of what you actually needed. It loses track of what matters, slipping important thoughts into the background until you are left wondering where the thread went and why it feels so hard to find again.

That's why you write it down.

A notebook. A calendar. A list. A whiteboard. A sticky note. A voice memo. A text to yourself. It does not have to be fancy. It just has to exist.

Get the thought out of your head and into a place you can see.

You are not being forgetful. You are being human.

And the more you try to hold everything in your head, the more your brain starts to feel foggy. Heavy. Like there are too many tabs open at once and nothing is loading properly.

Writing things down closes those tabs.

You do not have to keep refreshing your mind with reminders. You do not have to keep scanning your thoughts to make sure you are not missing anything. You can look at your list and know what is there. You can clear the noise and move forward.

That kind of clarity changes how your day feels.

It helps you sleep better. It helps you focus. It helps you be present, because you are not constantly trying to juggle invisible tasks and mental alarms.

Most people do not forget because they are careless. They forget because they tried to store too much in a system that is not built for long-term storage. Your brain is great at creativity, connection, and problem-solving. It is not great at remembering which bill is due on the 15th or which appointment got rescheduled or what you meant to pick up at the store.

That is what external memory is for.

When you write it down, you are giving yourself a safety net. You are creating something solid to catch the thought before it disappears. You are protecting your attention from unnecessary strain. You are no longer forcing your brain to keep juggling everything in the background. You are allowing your mind to rest. You are freeing it to focus on what it does best. You are giving it space to think clearly, instead of constantly trying to remember what not to forget. You are allowing your brain to rest and do what it's meant to do.

It also helps you follow through. When something is written down, it becomes more real. More visible. You are more likely to act on it, review it, or plan around it.

Without a list, everything floats around in your head, vague and unfinished. With a list, each task has form. It has order. It has a place to land.

Even simple notes can change the outcome of a day. One sentence in a notebook can become the idea that grows into something bigger. One reminder can save you from missing something important. One checklist can keep you on track when your energy dips and your mind feels scattered.

And the act of writing something down, physically or digitally, helps reinforce it. You remember it better. You stay more organized. You feel more capable, because you are not constantly chasing mental scraps.

It is also a kindness to others.

When you write things down, you are less likely to forget a promise. Less likely to miss a deadline. Less likely to make someone feel like they slipped through the cracks. You show respect by keeping track.

And when something slips your mind, because it still will from time to time, you have a record to come back to. You have something solid to check. You are not left guessing.

You are not relying on that vague feeling that something was on your list. That sense of *I think I was supposed to do something today* but can't remember what or when.

You are not left hoping the thought will come back on its own. You have it written. You can see it. You can trust it.

And that helps everyone. At work. At home. In your relationships. In your goals.

You do not have to have a perfect system. You do not have to organize like a productivity guru. You just have to create a habit of capturing what matters.

If a thought feels important, do not assume you will remember it later. Write it down now.

If a task needs to be done, do not leave it floating in your head. Add it to a list where it can live until it's finished.

If an idea excites you, do not let it fade. Give it a space. You can come back to it. You can build on it. But only if you remember it exists.

Do not make your brain carry the entire load.

The smartest people in the world use notes, reminders, and systems. Because they are human too. But they know better than to rely on memory alone.

It is not about being forgetful. It is about being prepared.

And when you write it down, you are not just organizing your tasks. You are organizing your mind. You are choosing clarity over chaos. You are deciding to be someone who follows through.

That kind of habit creates trust.

You trust yourself more. You feel more steady, more capable, more in control of your time and attention. Other people trust you more. They see that you follow through, that you remember what matters, that you show up prepared.

You are not constantly scrambling to remember what you promised. You are not trying to piece together where you need to be or what you said you would do. You are not chasing loose ends in your mind.

You become organized. Reliable. Dependable.

So write it down.

Even if you think you will remember.

Even if it seems small.

Even if you are sure it's obvious.

That is common sense.

Start Small, but Start

Big changes begin with small steps.

Everyone knows that, but most people still wait. They wait for the perfect time. They wait to feel ready. They wait for more motivation or better conditions or a day that feels just right.

But that day rarely comes.

You do not need a flawless plan. You do not need to overhaul your life. You just need to begin. Not with a leap, but with one small step. The smallest version of the thing you want to do. Something so simple it almost feels silly.

But it works.

Because once you begin, you are no longer thinking about it. You are doing it. You are moving. You are out of your head and into the real world.

The truth is, starting is often the hardest part. It looks like resistance. It feels like avoidance. But really, it's fear hiding under excuses. Fear of failing. Fear of not being good enough. Fear of looking foolish. Fear that the effort won't be worth it.

So we wait. We plan. We tweak the details. We search for the perfect system, the perfect routine, the perfect place to begin.

And the whole time, we are not moving. We are caught in the planning instead of the doing.

Start small instead.

If you want to get in shape, start with five push-ups. Not fifty. Just five.

If you want to read more, open the book and read one page. Not a whole chapter. Just one page.

If you want to clean your room, start with one corner. One drawer. One surface.

If you want to save money, set aside five dollars. Not five hundred. Just five.

The habit of starting is more valuable than the size of the step. It matters less how much you do and more that you begin. A small action done consistently will carry you further than a big effort you keep putting off.

Starting builds trust with yourself. It proves that you are willing to move, even when the step is small. And once you build the habit of starting, you can build almost anything on top of it. Every great achievement is simply a chain of small starts linked together.

When you start small, you give yourself something even better than progress. You give yourself momentum.

You remind yourself that action is possible. That you are not stuck. That you can move forward, even if it's just by an inch.

That inch matters.

One small step does not look like much, but it breaks the pattern of hesitation. It creates a shift. The task goes from "someday" to "in progress." That shift is where everything begins.

And once you have started, you can build. You can add more. You can adjust as you go. But none of that happens until you take that first small step.

You do not have to feel ready. You just have to begin.

Starting small also removes the pressure. You are not trying to change everything overnight. You are not trying to be perfect on day one. You are simply giving yourself permission to begin without the weight of unrealistic expectations.

And that's what keeps people stuck. They expect too much from the beginning.

They think the first workout has to be intense. The first draft has to be perfect. The first day of a new habit has to feel like a total transformation. And when it doesn't, they stop.

But you don't need transformation. You need movement.

Big outcomes are the result of small efforts repeated over time. Not once or twice, but again and again. It is the steady rhythm of showing up, even when progress feels slow. It is the quiet work that adds up when no one is watching. All lasting change is built this way.

And those efforts always begin with something tiny. A single action. A first step. Something so simple it might not even feel like progress. Something that feels almost too easy. But that small beginning is what opens the door.

That is the sweet spot. The place where resistance is low and momentum begins. The place where big goals stop feeling impossible and start to feel like something you can actually do.

Make your first step so small that you cannot fail. So simple that you have no excuse to avoid it.

You want to write a journal? Start with one sentence. You want to write a book? Open a blank page and type a single paragraph. You want to get organized? Clear off one shelf.

What matters is not how impressive the first step is. What matters is that you take it. That first step is not about progress. It is about permission. Once you begin, even in the smallest way, you prove to yourself that starting is possible.

And no, that step may not look like much from the outside. It may go unnoticed by others. It may not feel like a breakthrough. It may be quiet. It may be clumsy. It may be done in a corner of the day that no one sees. It may be messy. It may feel like barely anything at all.

But inside, it is a shift. Something changes. Something opens. You are no longer stuck in thought. You are no longer circling the idea in your head. It is the moment you move from waiting to doing. From delay to momentum. From hesitation to forward motion.

And that changes everything.

Start small, not because your goal is small, but because small is how everything big begins.

Nobody runs a marathon by sprinting the first mile. Nobody builds a strong habit in one day. Nobody wakes up with a new life because of one big effort.

People who finish big things don't start with big things. They start small. They show up. They keep going.

Small beginnings are not a weakness.

They are not a sign that you are unprepared or lacking. They are wisdom. They show that you understand how real progress is built. Slowly, steadily, one step at a time.

Small beginnings are sustainable.

You are not burning yourself out trying to do everything at once. You are moving at a pace you can maintain. You are laying a strong foundation.

Small beginnings are strong.

Not flashy or loud, but solid and dependable. Quiet strength that comes from consistency, not from rushing. They are honest about what it takes to grow something real. Growth is not instant. It is not clean or perfect. It takes time, patience, and small effort repeated again and again.

And if you stumble, you can recover. The fall is not far when the steps are small. If you miss a day, you can restart without shame. You are not starting over, just picking up where you left off. If you take a wrong turn, you are not far off course. You can adjust and return without feeling like you failed. That is the beauty of small beginnings. They leave you room to grow.

That is the power of small. You can keep going without burning out.

Most people do not need more motivation. They need less pressure. They need to let go of the idea that things must be impressive to be effective. They need to give themselves permission to begin badly, to begin slowly, to begin quietly.

But to begin.

You don't need a grand plan to get started. You don't need to see the whole path. You just need enough light to see where to place your foot next. Confidence grows from movement, not the other way around. Each small step builds the belief to take the next one.

You just need to take that first step. Even if it's shaky. Even if it feels small. Even if you are not sure where it will lead. Then take another. Just one more. Let your progress be measured in inches, not miles. Let it be quiet. Let it be uneven. Let it be enough.

Your confidence grows with action.

With each step, you prove to yourself that you can move forward. Your direction gets clearer as you move. The fog lifts a little. The next step becomes easier to see. Your energy picks up once you are no longer standing still. You start to build momentum. You start to feel capable. Not all at once, but gradually. One step at a time.

So whatever it is you have been putting off, begin. Do the small version. Do the easy version. Do the version that gets your hands moving and your mind engaged.

Because once you start, you are no longer stuck. You are building.

Everyday Habits

You are learning. You are changing.

You are doing the thing that most people never do. You are starting.

Start small, but start.

That is common sense.

Take Care of Things That Take Care of You

Some things are easy to take for granted. You use them every day. You rely on them without thinking. You expect them to work. You expect them to be there.

Until one day, they stop.

And then you realize just how much they were doing for you all along. You see how quietly they supported your days without asking for anything in return. You notice how many parts of your life depended on them running smoothly. What once felt invisible now feels essential.

That is why it matters to take care of the things that take care of you.

It sounds simple. But it runs deep.

Your body takes care of you. Every day, without asking for thanks. It carries you through your responsibilities. It keeps you upright. It helps you move, speak, eat, think, rest, recover, and endure. Even when you neglect it, it still tries to keep you going.

So take care of it.

Feed it well. Move it often. Let it sleep. Let it breathe. Notice when something feels off. Pay attention to pain instead of pushing through it. Do not punish it for not looking a certain way. Respect it for functioning, for holding you together, for doing its job in silence.

Your home takes care of you. Whether it's an apartment, a room, or an entire house, it's the place you return to when you are tired. It gives you shelter, privacy, a sense of safety. It holds your routines. It holds your rest. It reflects how you live.

So take care of it.

Clean it when it gets messy. Fix what breaks. Keep it functional. Keep it calm. You do not need to redecorate. You do not need to chase perfection. Just respect it enough not to let it fall apart. Even the smallest space can feel peaceful when it's cared for.

Your tools take care of you. Your phone, your computer, your car, your clothes, your shoes, your kitchen items. These are the things that help you function. They help you work, communicate, move, and meet your needs. And like anything, they wear down when neglected.

So take care of them.

Update your software. Get the oil change. Wipe the screen. Polish the shoes. Tighten the loose screw. Charge the battery before it runs dry. Keep your gear in good condition, even if it seems like a small thing. Because those small things add up.

The better you treat your tools, the longer they last. They work better and cause fewer problems. You spend less time fixing and more time using them for what they were meant to do. And the smoother your life runs as a result.

It is not about being obsessive. It's about giving a little care before small problems become big ones.

You do not need to be perfect or meticulous. It is about avoiding stress that you could have prevented with simple upkeep. Just a little attention here and there saves you from bigger problems down the road.

Your relationships take care of you. They hold you up when life feels heavy. They remind you who you are when you start to forget. The people you talk to, the ones you trust, are the ones who make the hard days softer and the good days brighter.

The ones who support you without needing to be asked. The ones who listen without judgment. The ones who check in, help out, sit with you, laugh with you. The ones who make space for your thoughts, your mess, your joy, your struggle.

The ones who keep you grounded when things are hard. They do not always have answers, but they stay. They remind you that you are not alone. That your life is bigger than the moment you are stuck in.

So take care of them.

Say thank you. Say sorry. Show up. Respond to the message. Remember their birthday. Ask how they are doing. Relationships need maintenance too. Not grand gestures, just presence. Just a little effort. Just the reminder that you see them and value them.

Your routines take care of you. The small, steady things you do without thinking. Brushing your teeth. Making your bed. Moving your body. Getting outside. Drinking water. They keep your days from falling apart when everything else feels uncertain.

So take care of them.

Do not wait until you feel motivated. Protect your routines, especially when life gets busy. They are the scaffolding that holds you together when things wobble. The structure that carries you through without needing to think too hard. Simple habits, done consistently, are some of the strongest forms of support you have.

Even your space, your schedule, your quiet moments all take care of you in small ways. They shape how you feel, how you think, and how you move through the day. A calm room can bring you a sense of peace. A steady routine can give your mind something to lean on when everything else feels uncertain. A quiet moment can reset your thoughts and remind you to breathe. These are small things, but they carry real weight.

That walk you take to clear your head. That ten minutes of silence before the day starts. That unread message you give yourself permission not to open yet. These things are not luxuries. They are forms of care. They keep you steady. They help you recover.

And like anything else, they need your attention. Not constantly. But regularly.

If something is taking care of you, return the favor. Whether it's your body, your home, your tools, or your relationships, give back to what supports you. Maintain it. Clean it. Nurture it. Do not wait until it breaks down, wears out, or disappears to realize how much it mattered. Care is easiest when it's consistent. Small effort now prevents big problems later. Respect what helps you by treating it like it matters before it forces you to.

It is easy to ignore the oil light until the engine groans. You tell yourself it can wait. You assume it's not urgent. Then one day, the damage is louder than the warning ever was.

It is easy to push through pain until your body says enough. You brush it off. You convince yourself you can handle it. Then suddenly, the discomfort turns into something you cannot ignore.

It is easy to neglect the friendship until the silence feels too wide to cross. At first it's just a missed message. Then a delayed reply. Then the habit of not reaching out becomes the new normal. And before you know it, the connection that once felt natural now feels distant.

But it doesn't have to get to that point.

You can act before the damage. You can maintain instead of repair. You can be someone who looks after what matters before it falls apart.

This kind of care is not flashy. It is quiet. It is steady. It happens in the background, often unnoticed. But it makes everything else run more smoothly.

When you take care of what takes care of you, you suffer less. You scramble less. You recover faster. You feel stronger. You feel more comfortable. Not because everything is perfect, but because you are not ignoring the basics.

Do not wait until crisis to pay attention.

This kind of care is not about control. It is about respect. It is about gratitude. You are saying, *This matters to me. This helps me. I will treat it like it does.*

And no, you will not always get it right. Things slip. Life gets hectic. We all forget. But when you notice yourself slipping, come back to this. Come back to the habit of care.

Do the small thing now instead of the big thing later. Tidy the space instead of letting it collapse. Stretch the body instead of waiting for the injury. Send the text instead of losing touch. Sharpen the knife instead of throwing it out. Recharge the battery before it dies.

These are not chores. These are acts of responsibility. And more than that, they are acts of wisdom.

You are not wasting time by taking care of what supports you. You are saving time. You are saving stress. You are making your life lighter.

When you care for your tools, your relationships, your home, your routines, and your body, you create an environment that supports you back.

It becomes easier to focus. Easier to rest. Easier to move forward.

Because you are not constantly fixing what you could have preserved.

When you give back to what supports you, life gives back to you.

Take care of things that take care of you.

That is common sense.

PART THREE

People and Relationships

People and Relationships

Life is shaped by the way we treat each other. Listening shows respect. Boundaries protect both sides. Kindness often reaches further than cleverness. Honesty matters because trust cannot grow without it. The way you speak, the patience you offer, and the promises you keep are the things people carry with them. This chapter is about leaving marks that heal instead of wounds that last.

Be Kinder Than Necessary: People Are Fighting Battles You Can't See

Be kinder than necessary: people are fighting battles you can't see.

It is probably not the first time you have heard it. It is one of those sayings that floats around, pinned to bulletin boards, shared on social media, repeated by well-meaning people. But do not let the familiarity fool you. It is not just good advice. It is a way of seeing the world.

Because here is what no one tells you: most people are hurting.

Not all the time. Not always in loud or visible ways. But underneath the surface, behind the polite smiles and the quick small talk, people are carrying things. Big things. Quiet things. Private grief. Constant anxiety. Overwhelming pressure. Hidden loneliness. And you almost never see it.

You pass hundreds of people a day. A barista. A co-worker. A stranger in traffic. Someone at the gym. A classmate. A neighbor. A cashier. Behind every one of them is a life that is full of complexity. Messy, unpredictable, shaped by things you will never know about. Some of them are hanging on by a thread. Some are putting on a brave face. Some are trying to survive the next five minutes.

They do not wear signs. They do not announce it. But the weight is there.

And that is where kindness becomes everything.

Not the fake smile kind. Not the check-the-box kind. Not the type that shows up when people are watching. I am talking about real kindness. The kind that sees people as human. The kind that pauses instead of reacting. The kind that chooses patience instead of assumption. The kind that asks nothing in return.

Sometimes it is small. Holding the door. Saying thank you and meaning it. Letting someone merge in traffic without needing a wave of acknowledgment. Texting a friend just to say you are thinking of them. Speaking with softness instead of sarcasm. Forgiving before you are asked. Choosing to give someone the benefit of the doubt.

None of these are heroic on their own. They are small, everyday gestures. Easy to overlook. Easy to skip. But to someone who is struggling, even the smallest act can land like a lifeline. It can feel like a hand reaching out in the dark. Like a quiet reminder that they are not invisible. Like proof that the world is not entirely cold.

A kind word might interrupt a spiral of self-doubt. A gentle tone might calm a storm no one else can see. A moment of patience might be the one thing that keeps someone from breaking down. You never really know what these simple moments might mean to someone else.

But they often mean more than you could imagine.

One story I have never forgotten: a man stood in line at the grocery store. Nothing about him stood out. He stared at the floor, groceries in hand. Quiet. Still. The woman behind him noticed his hands were shaking slightly. When he looked up, she smiled. A small, honest smile. Nothing dramatic. He nodded, paid for his things, and left.

After he walked out, the cashier leaned in and whispered, "His wife passed away last week. That was their grocery store. First time he came in without her."

That woman had no way of knowing. But her kindness still mattered. It did not fix anything. It did not take away the pain. But it landed. It reminded him that the world had not gone completely cold.

And that is the point. Kindness is not about waiting for people to earn it. It is about giving it anyway, especially when you do not know how much it is needed. Because you never really know. You never know who just got bad news. Who is struggling with a decision they cannot talk about. Who is feeling invisible, or ashamed, or afraid. You do not need a reason to be gentle.

The truth is, life is heavy for most people in different ways. Some carry it with a smile. Some bury it beneath busyness. Some crack under the pressure. No one escapes it entirely. So when someone acts impatient, cold, distant, or even rude, try not to assume the worst. Try asking yourself, just for a second, what they might be carrying that you cannot see.

That moment of curiosity can change everything.

And no, you might never know the answer. You might never get closure or clarity. But you will have chosen to be part of the solution instead of the noise. You will have made a moment softer when it could have easily turned sharp.

Let us be clear: kindness does not mean being a doormat. It does not mean tolerating disrespect or avoiding boundaries. It does not mean letting people walk all over you. You can be clear and still be kind. You can be firm and still be kind. You can disagree, even strongly, and still be kind.

Kindness is not weakness.

Kindness is not passive. It is not soft in the way people think. It is strength under control. It is the ability to stay grounded when someone else is losing it. It is the decision not to meet fire with fire. It is the quiet confidence that says, "I do not have to match your energy. I can lead with mine."

You do not do it because you expect applause. You do not do it to be better than someone. You do it because you know that pain hides well. That people are layered. That today might not be someone's best day. And that you have had days like that too.

You've had mornings where you barely held it together. Nights where you cried alone and hoped no one would notice. Moments when you lashed out or shut down or said something you did not mean, just because your heart was too heavy. And if someone gave you patience on one of those days, if someone looked at you with compassion instead of judgment, you remember that.

You remember it in your body. In your chest. In your gut. You remember how it made you feel less alone.

So be that for someone else. Be the one who softens the moment. Be the one who doesn't escalate. Be the one who stays kind even when it would be easier not to.

You will not regret it.

You will not lie awake wishing you had been colder or harsher. You will not look back and wish you had snapped more. But you will remember the moments when you were the steady one. The kind one. The human one.

And sometimes, weeks or months later, someone will tell you that your words stayed with them. That your patience made them feel safe. That your presence helped them breathe. And even if no one ever tells you, even if you never know what difference you made, it still matters.

Because kindness changes people. Quietly. Slowly. Steadily. It opens doors in others, and it opens doors in you. It rewires how you see the world. It slows you down. It makes you curious instead of reactive. It softens your voice. It changes how you show up when it matters most.

And no, not everyone will appreciate it. Some people will still be rude. Some will take advantage. Some will not notice at all. That's okay.

Because you are not doing it just for them. You are also doing it for you. You are doing it because you have decided to be the kind of person who adds light. The kind of person who does not contribute to the mess. The kind of person who believes that softness still matters, even in a loud and fast and hard world.

Someone has to go first. Let it be you.

Be kind when it's easy.

Be kind when it's hard.

Be kind when someone else is not.

Be kind when no one is watching.

Be kind when it feels pointless.

Be kind for no reason at all.

And then take it one step further.

Be kinder than necessary.

Kindness costs you little and might mean everything to someone else.

That is common sense.

You Teach People How to Treat You

You teach people how to treat you.

At first, that might sound like an oversimplification, a catchy little phrase you would find on a coffee mug or a social media post. But sit with it for a moment. Because buried in those few words is one of the quiet truths that shapes your entire life.

Look at the way people interact with you. The way people speak to you. The way they respond to your needs. The way they show up, or do not, in your relationships.

That behavior doesn't happen in a vacuum. It is shaped, in part, by what you allow. What you tolerate. What you reinforce, even unintentionally.

Without realizing it, you are setting the standard. But most of us do not see ourselves as "teachers" in our daily lives.

We are just trying to get through the day, show up, be decent, keep the peace. But whether you realize it or not, you are constantly sending messages about what is acceptable. Every shrug. Every forced laugh. Every *It's fine* when it's really not. Every time you bite your tongue to avoid conflict. Every time you stay silent because you don't want to seem "too sensitive." That is communication. That is instruction. You are teaching people how to treat you.

It starts small. Maybe someone makes a sarcastic joke at your expense. You feel a sting, but you don't want to seem sensitive, so you force a laugh. No harm done, right? But next time, it's a little sharper. A little more public. And because you never said anything the first time, they assume it's fair game. The longer it goes on, the harder it becomes to speak up. And now what started as "just a joke" has become a pattern.

That's how most of these things begin. Not with big moments, but with little ones. And if you are not careful, those little moments pile up into a dynamic that doesn't feel good, doesn't feel fair, and doesn't reflect who you are or how you want to be treated.

Now, this doesn't mean you're responsible for how others behave. Some people will push boundaries no matter what you do. But you are responsible for what you accept, what you ignore, and what you reinforce. And that matters. A lot.

Think about the people in your life who set clear boundaries. You probably know someone like that. They do not raise their voice. They are not cold. They are not confrontational. But they have a calm, steady presence that says, without words, they are not someone to mess with. They do not tolerate passive-aggressive digs. They do not overextend themselves to be liked. They do not explain their "no" five different ways just to soften the blow. And they do not let people take advantage of their time, their energy, or their kindness.

But here is the thing: they are not unkind. In fact, they are probably very kind. Generous, even. Supportive, thoughtful, good to be around. The difference is that their kindness doesn't come at the cost of self-respect. They know where the line is, and they do not let people cross it.

People tend to treat them with more care, more attention, more respect. Not out of fear, but because they know exactly where the line is. There is no guessing. No testing the waters to see how far they can push. The boundaries are there, firm, quiet, visible, and that shapes the entire dynamic.

That kind of presence does not happen by accident. It is a decision. A practiced one. It is someone who has done the inner work to understand their own limits, who has learned (maybe the hard way) that saying yes to everything leaves you drained, resentful, and stretched thin. It is someone who has realized that self-respect doesn't just protect you, it teaches others how to engage with you.

We respect people who respect themselves.

It is that simple. And when someone shows you, not just with words but with actions, that they value their time, their space, and their peace, you naturally fall in line. Not because they demand it, but because they model it.

And it's a choice you can make too.

You don't have to yell. You don't have to lecture. You don't have to make a scene or draw a line in the sand in front of an audience. You don't need to prove a point or launch into a long speech about boundaries and respect. It doesn't have to be dramatic, and it doesn't have to be loud.

But it does have to be clear.

You do have to decide, quietly and firmly, what you are willing to tolerate and what you are not. You have to get honest with yourself about what feels okay and what does not. About what drains you. What crosses a line. What leaves you feeling small, or used, or invisible. And once you know that, you have to act on it.

Sometimes that means speaking up in the moment. Sometimes it means changing how you respond, or distancing yourself, or letting a relationship fade out. But the first step is always the same: choosing not to ignore it anymore.

If you do not draw the line, no one will know it exists.

And if you keep moving it to make others comfortable, one day you will not even remember where it was meant to be. The boundary that once protected you will blur until it disappears. By the time you notice, it may be too late.

If someone keeps canceling plans at the last minute, and you always shrug it off and rearrange your schedule, guess what happens next time? They cancel again. Not because they're evil or malicious. But because you've taught them that your time doesn't need to be respected.

If a coworker dumps his work on you and you keep picking up the slack without saying a word, you're teaching him that it's okay to treat you like a safety net. If a friend only calls when she needs something, and you keep saying yes, you're teaching her that your relationship doesn't need to be mutual.

You can un-teach people too. Although this is harder, because it means breaking patterns that have already been built. It takes consistency, and sometimes people will resist the change. But over time, they learn from your new boundaries just as they learned from your old ones.

You can reset the pattern and show up differently. It starts with choosing new responses, even in small moments. Little shifts can change the whole dynamic.

It starts with one firm sentence, said calmly. You pause instead of laughing off the rude comment. You say, "That didn't sit right with me." You let someone know, kindly but firmly, that your time matters too. You don't make excuses for other people's disrespect. You stop over-explaining your boundaries, and you start trusting that they're valid, even if someone doesn't like them.

And yes, it's uncomfortable. Especially at first. Especially if you're used to being agreeable or accommodating or easygoing. Especially if you were raised to keep the peace.

But here's the tradeoff: every time you speak up for yourself, you strengthen your sense of worth. You start attracting people who actually respect you, not just tolerate you.

Sometimes people will push back. They will say you have changed. That you are being cold or difficult. That you are overreacting. That is not about you. That is about them losing access to the version of you that did not have boundaries. And if they cannot handle the new version, one with more self-respect, that tells you something important.

You deserve relationships where you feel safe. Where your voice matters. Where your time is valued. Where kindness goes both ways. And that doesn't happen by accident. It happens by design. You create the dynamic you want by how you show up, what you say yes to, and what you let go of.

There is a quote that floats around sometimes. It says, "No one will ever treat you better than you treat yourself." It sounds cheesy, but it's real. The way you talk about yourself, the way you show up for yourself, the way you advocate for your needs, that sets the tone for how others treat you. If you act like your time does not matter, others will believe you. If you act like your feelings are not important, others will believe that too.

So treat yourself like someone worth respecting. Start there. The rest tends to follow.

And remember, teaching people how to treat you isn't about being controlling. It's not about manipulating people into behaving a certain way. It's about honesty. It's about clarity. It's about showing up with self-awareness and saying, "This is who I am. This is how I expect to be treated. And this is what I won't allow."

Some people will rise to meet you. Others will fall away. Both outcomes are okay.

Because when you stop tolerating disrespect, when you stop laughing off discomfort, when you stop shrinking to make others more comfortable, you create space for something better. For relationships that actually nourish you. For friendships that feel mutual. For environments that feel safe.

You teach people how to treat you.

So teach them well.

This is common sense.

Don't Interrupt

Don't interrupt... It sounds simple. Basic manners. The kind of thing most of us were taught as kids. But in practice, it's one of the most overlooked and underappreciated habits in everyday life. And it's one of the clearest signs of respect. Or lack of it.

When someone is speaking and you cut them off, even if you don't mean to, the message they receive is this: *what I'm saying doesn't matter as much as what you want to say.*

It doesn't feel good. You have felt it yourself.

You are mid-thought, trying to explain something. Maybe it's personal. Maybe it's complicated. You are still figuring out how to say it. And just as you start to feel like you are being heard, the other person jumps in. They offer advice you were not asking for. They cut in with disagreement before you even finish. They make a joke. Or worse, they shift the focus to themselves. They tell their own story and leave yours hanging in the air, unfinished.

And just like that, the moment changes.

You are no longer part of the conversation. You are on the outside, watching it move on without you. The space where you were opening up now feels smaller. Less safe.

You go quiet. You back away. Not because you have nothing left to say, but because the invitation to say it disappeared.

We all do it, sometimes without realizing. The words pop into our head and we want to say them before we forget. Or we are sure we already know where the other person is going. Or we get excited. Or impatient. Or we assume what we have to say is more interesting, more accurate, more helpful.

But interrupting someone, even with good intentions, is rarely received well. Because it interrupts more than a sentence. It interrupts the flow of trust. It turns a dialogue into a tug-of-war. And once trust is broken, the words matter less.

One of the most powerful things you can offer someone is your full attention. That means letting them finish. Letting them stumble through their thoughts if needed. Letting the silence sit for a moment instead of rushing to fill it. It means listening not just for your turn to speak, but to actually understand.

Think about the best conversations you have had. The ones where you felt truly heard.

Chances are, the other person did not interrupt you. They let you speak without rushing you. They stayed with you through the pauses and the rambling. They listened not just to your words, but to what you meant. They asked thoughtful questions that showed they were paying attention. They did not jump in to fix, correct, or take over. They stayed present.

They let the moment be yours.

They didn't hijack your story. They didn't make it about them. They gave you room to find your words and time to land your thought. And because of that, something opened up.

That moment felt like respect.

And that respect made you feel safe. Safe enough to go deeper. Safe enough to say what you really meant. Safe enough to trust them with a little more of yourself.

We live in a world that rewards speed. Quick answers, fast takes, short attention spans. But relationships aren't built on speed. They're built on patience. And listening is the foundation.

Imagine your friend is telling you about a rough day at work. Halfway through, you jump in: "You should talk to your boss." Or, "That happened to me once. Let me tell you what I did." You are trying to help. But they were not looking for a solution. They just wanted to be heard.

Now they have lost their train of thought, and you have unknowingly shifted the spotlight. That moment to connect? Gone. All because you could not wait ten more seconds. Ten seconds can be the difference between connection and distance.

When you don't interrupt someone, especially when it's hard not to, it sends a strong message: *I care about what you're saying. I respect your thoughts. I value you.*

And the truth is, most people are not looking for someone to fix their problem or outdo their story. They are just looking to be heard. To feel like someone is really, truly paying attention. If you can give someone your full, uninterrupted presence, you are giving them something rare. The feeling of being truly heard.

Now, this doesn't mean you can't ever speak up. It doesn't mean you have to sit in silence or let conversations drag endlessly. But there's a rhythm to good communication. And that rhythm starts with restraint.

Let people finish. Let them breathe. Let the moment land before you jump in.

Now picture a team meeting.

Someone is presenting an idea. They have just started laying it out. They are a few points in, still building toward the core of what they want to say. And then a colleague interrupts. Not rudely, not loudly. But abruptly enough to shift the tone.

"Yeah, but we already tried something like that last year."

Maybe the comment is valid. Maybe it even needs to be said. But the timing breaks the flow. The presenter freezes for a second. They lose their momentum.

Now they are on the defensive.

They scramble to explain why this time is different. Others in the room start reacting, not listening. People check out or jump in. The conversation that could have been thoughtful now feels like a tug-of-war.

And it all started with one person who could not wait thirty more seconds.

There's also this: sometimes we interrupt because we're uncomfortable. With silence. With emotion. With disagreement. So we cut in. We lighten the mood. We steer things in a direction that feels safer. But when we do that, we miss something important. We miss the part of the conversation that mattered most. The part they needed you to hear.

Sometimes the most respectful thing you can do is stay quiet and listen. Really listen. Say nothing at all.

This is especially important in conflict. When you're upset, or when the other person is. Interrupting in those moments feels like an attack. It turns a conversation into a competition. Everyone starts talking louder, faster, trying to be heard, and no one actually is. But if even one person stays calm and listens, really listens, the whole tone shifts.

Listening does not mean agreeing.

Letting someone finish does not mean you think they are right. It just means you are offering them the basic dignity of being heard before you speak. You are showing respect by allowing their thoughts to land before adding your own.

And that changes everything.

Sometimes the tension people bring into a conversation is not about the topic. It is about feeling ignored. It is about feeling like no one is really listening. So when you let someone speak without cutting in, something shifts.

They start to relax.

They do not need to raise their voice. They do not need to fight to be heard. And once they say what they needed to say, they often soften.

Because being heard is often what people are really after.

There is a difference between hearing and waiting to speak. One is about connection. The other makes people feel unheard.

You do not have to be the loudest voice in the room to be respected. Often, it's the quiet ones, the ones who listen first and speak with intention, that carry the most weight. Because people remember how you made them feel. And being listened to feels good. It feels uncommon. It feels like care.

So next time you feel the urge to interrupt, pause. Let them finish their thought. Even if you disagree. Even if you already know what they're going to say. Even if you're sure you have something more helpful or accurate or clever.

Let them speak. Then speak.

It is not flashy. It won't get applause. But it will change your relationships. It will change how people experience you. And it will make you someone others feel safe around.

That's the quiet power of not interrupting.

The kind of power that turns a team meeting into progress instead of politics.

The kind that lets a friend finish their story.

The kind that earns trust without saying a word.

That is common sense.

Say What You Mean, but Don't Say It Mean

Some people speak their mind like they are throwing punches. Every thought comes out fast, sharp, and unfiltered. The words might be true, but the way they land leaves bruises.

Others barely speak at all, even when it matters most. They hold their feelings in, swallow their reactions, and hope someone else will guess what is wrong. But silence creates its own kind of damage.

The skill that builds connection lives in the middle. Say what you mean, but don't say it mean.

On one side are the people who say everything that crosses their mind, completely unfiltered, like a verbal fire hose. They speak fast, sharp, and often loud. They will tell you they are "just being honest" or "calling it like they see it," as if honesty automatically makes something helpful.

More often than not, the honesty is coated in judgment, frustration, or ego. The words may be technically true, but the delivery leaves bruises.

It feels less like a conversation and more like an ambush.

And when the dust settles, it's clear the truth did not bring anyone closer. It only left people guarded or hurt.

On the other side are the people who do the opposite. They hold everything in. They swallow their reactions, minimize their feelings, and sidestep anything uncomfortable. They sugarcoat their disappointment. They avoid confrontation.

Sometimes they stay quiet because they do not want to seem dramatic. Other times they are afraid of rocking the boat or being misunderstood.

They do not want to hurt anyone. But in trying so hard to avoid conflict, they end up building distance. Or resentment. Or both.

Eventually, the pressure builds. Then things either explode or fade into silence.

Neither of these extremes creates healthy relationships. One hurts people. The other hides from them. One shuts doors. The other leaves them half-open, never fully crossed. And both leave everyone feeling misunderstood.

The real skill, the one that actually builds connection, lives in the middle. It is the ability to speak your truth with care. To be honest, but not harsh. To say the thing that matters, but in a way that someone else can actually hear it.

It is not about softening your message until it loses meaning. It is about respecting your voice and theirs at the same time. It is about balancing clarity with compassion.

That balance does not happen by accident. It takes awareness. It takes intention. It takes practice.

Once you find it, everything changes. Because now you are not just saying what is true. You are saying it in a way that keeps the relationship intact.

This is when it matters most to speak clearly and directly. Say what you mean. Do not be vague. Do not expect people to read your mind. Do not dance around something important and then feel frustrated when no one picks up on the clues.

If it matters, say it. Say it clearly. Say it calmly. Say it with confidence.

But don't say it mean.

Because how you say something matters just as much as what you say. Tone matters. Timing matters. Intention matters. The delivery can completely change the meaning.

People and Relationships

You can have the most honest, necessary truth in the world, but if you say it with sarcasm, spite, or a raised voice, it won't land. It will sting. It will trigger defenses. It will make the other person shut down instead of open up.

You can speak the truth, and still speak it with kindness. That's not weakness, it's wisdom. In fact, it's often the kindness that allows the truth to land at all. When you say something with warmth, patience, and clarity, you create a space where the other person feels safe enough to hear it. They might not agree with you. They might not like what you said. But they won't feel attacked. And that makes all the difference.

Kindness does not dilute the truth. It delivers it more effectively. It lowers the emotional volume so the message can be heard. It says: *I care enough to tell you, and I care enough not to crush you with it.*

Kindness makes space for the other person to actually listen.

You can be clear without being cold. You can be honest without being harsh. And you can speak directly without speaking down.

That's what it means to say what you mean without saying it mean.

Think about a time someone gave you hard feedback. The kind that made you pause. Maybe even flinch. Maybe they told you that you were being unfair. Or they pointed out a blind spot. Or they asked you to change something you had not realized was a problem.

It probably was not a comfortable moment. But if they said it in a way that felt respectful, if their tone was calm and their words were thoughtful, something in you stayed open. You could tell they were not trying to tear you down. They were coming from a place of care. They wanted to help, not hurt.

Because of that, you listened. You might not have agreed right away, but the message landed. It stuck. Maybe it changed the way you saw things.

Respect does not water down the truth. It makes it possible to hear it.

Now think about the same kind of feedback, but delivered differently. Imagine it said with sarcasm. Or in front of other people. Imagine it laced with frustration, or spoken in a cold, clipped tone that made you feel small.

Suddenly, the words do not matter as much. Your attention shifts to how it made you feel. You stop hearing the message and start hearing the judgment.

Even if the point was valid, the delivery shut the door. Instead of reflection, you feel defensive. Instead of understanding, you feel tension.

The conversation, which could have led to something better, now feels like a wall instead of a window.

The difference isn't just the content. It is the delivery. It is the energy behind the words. The same truth, spoken with care, builds trust. The same truth, spoken with edge, breaks it.

How you say something can either build a bridge or burn one down.

We often forget that. We think: *Well, I was just being honest.* As if honesty alone excuses delivery. But there's a difference between being honest and being hurtful. One invites conversation. The other shuts it down.

And let's be honest, most of the time we know when our tone is sharp. We know when we are being snappy, or passive-aggressive, or a little too blunt. Maybe we are tired. Or annoyed. Or trying to make a point.

Part of growing up emotionally is learning how to feel all of that and still choose to communicate with respect.

Saying what you mean doesn't mean you get to unload on people. It means you get to speak your truth in a way that's rooted in self-respect, not ego. You don't need to yell to be heard. You don't need to cut someone down to make your point. And you definitely don't need to be "mean" just to prove you're being "real."

You can say, "That really upset me," without shouting.

You can say, "I need some space," without slamming a door.

You can say, "This isn't working for me," without making the other person feel like a failure.

You can be honest without being cruel.

It takes practice. It takes pausing before you speak. It takes asking yourself, *How would I want to hear this if the roles were reversed?* And sometimes, it takes walking away and coming back later, once the heat of the moment has passed.

But it is worth it. Because when people know you will speak your truth and do it with care, they trust you more. They feel safer around you. They listen better. They open up more.

That kind of communication strengthens relationships. It creates clarity instead of confusion. Connection instead of conflict.

It builds bridges instead of walls, and gives both people a chance to feel heard.

And it goes both ways. The more you speak with kindness, the more you start to expect it in return. You stop accepting sarcasm as closeness. You stop mistaking meanness for strength. You start surrounding yourself with people who can handle honesty and still be gentle with your heart.

That's the sweet spot. That's where respect lives.

And sometimes it's not even about conflict. Sometimes it's about the little things. Like saying thank you sincerely. Like telling someone you appreciate them before it's too late. Like expressing what you need instead of dropping hints. Like being able to say, "I was wrong," or "I am sorry," without turning it into a performance or a defense.

This is what healthy communication looks like. It is truthful but gentle, clear but respectful.

It is not always easy. Sometimes your emotions will want to take the wheel. Anger. Frustration. Hurt. And in those moments, it feels good, at least for a little while, to lash out, to say the sharp thing, to make your point sting. But that satisfaction fades quickly. And what is left is regret. Distance. Damage.

So take the pause.

Choose the version of your truth that's still true, but gentler. Still clear, but kinder.

Say what you mean.

But don't say it mean.

Say it with care.

That is the kind of truth people remember.

That is common sense.

Listen More Than You Talk

We all want to be heard. To feel like our voice matters. That someone is really listening, not just waiting for their turn to speak, but actually taking in what we're saying. And yet, so many conversations feel more like two people taking turns than two people truly connecting.

That's why the simplest advice often makes the biggest difference: listen more than you talk.

At first, it sounds obvious. Listen more than you talk. It is the kind of advice your grandmother probably told you. It feels simple, like something everyone already knows. But in real conversations, it's harder than it seems.

Listening takes effort. It takes intention.

It means putting your own thoughts on pause long enough to make room for someone else's. It means focusing fully on the person in front of you, not just nodding while you plan what you're going to say next. Most people are only half-listening while they wait for their turn to speak. Real listening asks for more than silence. It asks for presence.

To really listen, you have to slow yourself down. You have to stop racing ahead in your mind. You have to stop treating conversations like a game where the goal is to be the smartest or the fastest. Listening means showing up fully, not just with your ears, but with your attention.

Listening means staying curious instead of assuming you already know what the other person is trying to say. It means giving someone space to finish, even when you think you've heard it all before. Because what they are saying might not be new to you, but it might be hard for them to say. And if you rush in too soon, you might miss something that really matters.

In many conversations, people are not truly listening. They are waiting. Waiting to jump in with their opinion. Waiting to give advice. Waiting to tell their story or prove their point. On the surface, they look engaged. They nod at the right moments. They murmur responses like "yeah" or "totally" or "I get that." They might even repeat a few of your words to make it seem like they are following along.

But underneath all of that, their mind is moving fast. They are not sitting with what you are saying. They are planning what they will say next. They are lining up their response, building their counterargument, or thinking about how what you are saying relates to them.

And the moment you pause long enough, they jump in. Not because they do not care, but because they were never really with you to begin with. They were just waiting for their turn.

You can feel it when someone is doing that to you. And it never feels good.

On the other hand, when someone actually listens, really listens, it's powerful. They're not trying to fix you. They're not interrupting or correcting or drifting off halfway through your sentence. They're with you. That kind of attention is rare. And that's exactly why it's so valuable.

One of the most respectful things you can do in any relationship is to give someone your presence. Not your opinion. Not your solution. Just your presence.

When someone is sharing something personal, or emotional, or even just frustrating, resist the urge to take over the moment.

You don't need to top their story with one of your own. You don't need to play therapist or offer twelve solutions. You don't even need to understand it completely. You just need to stay there long enough for them to feel heard.

That alone makes a difference.

Think about the last time you had a lot on your mind. You went to someone hoping they would understand, or at least care. If they gave you advice too quickly, or minimized how you felt, or kept checking their phone, it probably did not help.

But if they sat with you, nodded gently, gave you space to get your thoughts out, and asked questions out of curiosity rather than judgment, that probably helped more than anything they could have said.

That's the quiet power of listening. It doesn't always solve the problem. It doesn't erase what someone is going through or magically fix their situation. But it gives them something just as important. It gives them the strength to face it.

When someone feels heard, they feel less alone.

When people can speak freely without being cut off or judged, they start to untangle their own thoughts. The weight they are carrying might still be heavy, but it feels a little more manageable.

Sometimes the simple act of being listened to, fully, patiently, and without interruption, is the thing that reminds a person they can keep going. It tells them that their voice matters, that their story is worth the time it takes to share. It tells them that they are not invisible to you. It tells them that you respect them.

And yes, listening takes patience. Especially when the person speaking is going on longer than you'd like. Or repeating themselves. Or struggling to explain what they mean. The easy thing is to cut them off. Finish their sentence. Shift the topic. But easy isn't always right.

Give people room.

Give them room to fumble, to reflect, to find the words. Don't rush to fill every silence.

Some of the most meaningful moments happen in the quiet that follows what someone didn't quite know how to say.

Listening also means putting your ego aside. It means not turning every conversation into a mirror where you insert your own story. It means staying curious instead of assuming you already know what they are going to say. It means letting someone be the center of attention for a while, not because you are unimportant, but because it's not your moment.

If you want stronger relationships in your personal life, your work life, and your family, listen more. That alone will set you apart. People naturally gravitate toward those who make them feel heard.

Listening builds trust. It creates space for honesty. When people feel truly listened to, they open up in ways they usually don't. They feel safer, more connected, and more willing to meet you halfway. That kind of connection holds up under pressure.

There is a reason we're given two ears and one mouth. The proportions matter.

Of course, none of this means your voice doesn't matter. Your words carry more power when they come after you've listened.

Listening more than you talk doesn't mean you should stay quiet forever or keep your thoughts to yourself. Your voice matters. Your perspective matters.

There is a time to speak. A time to step in. A time to offer your insight or your story or whatever is sitting on your heart. But that moment lands with more impact when it comes after you've truly listened.

When people around you feel heard, they're more willing to hear you in return. Your words carry more weight when they're not competing for attention but arriving as part of a shared space.

Speaking without listening feels like noise. But speaking after listening feels like contribution.

This is especially true when there is disagreement. When emotions are high or opinions are divided, people naturally get defensive. They brace for a fight.

But if you show that you are actually listening, not pretending and not simply waiting for your turn to respond, everything changes. The tension drops. The room softens. What could have become an argument becomes a conversation.

You don't have to agree with someone to treat them with respect.

You don't have to see the world the same way to hear them out. But if you want others to respect you, the starting point is simple. You have to listen first.

The best communicators are not the ones who talk the most. They are not the ones filling every silence or dominating every exchange. They are the ones who make people feel safe to speak. They are the ones who listen closely enough that others feel understood.

So try this: in your next conversation, aim to listen just a little longer than feels natural. Pause before jumping in. Let the other person fully finish their thought. Let a silence hang in the air instead of rushing to fill it. You might be surprised at what they say when given space and at how much stronger your connection becomes.

Because in the end, listening is one of the most generous things you can offer. It doesn't cost a thing, but it makes people feel valued.

Listening makes people feel understood. It makes them feel heard. And often, that's what they needed more than your advice, your opinion, or your solution.

Talk less.

Listen more.

Not to stay quiet, but to hear better. Not to disappear, but to understand.

That isn't profound.

That isn't complicated.

That is common sense.

Apologize When You're Wrong: It's Strength, Not Weakness

Apologize when you're wrong. It's strength, not weakness.

"I'm sorry." Two simple words. But we don't say them often enough.

Those simple words hold more power than they seem to. They can completely shift how people experience you. But more importantly, they can shift how you experience yourself. When you start to see apologizing as an act of integrity rather than defeat, something changes. You stop feeling small for admitting your mistakes. You start feeling steady, clear, and anchored. You realize you do not have to be perfect in order to be respected, only honest.

For some reason, a lot of people think saying sorry means giving something up. As if it's an admission of defeat. A sign that you've lost power. That you're somehow smaller or weaker now. But in reality, the opposite is true.

A sincere apology, offered with clarity and humility, is one of the strongest, most human things you can do. It means you value the relationship more than your pride. It means you care enough about the other person to own your part in what went wrong.

Everyone messes up. That's just part of life.

We all say things we wish we could take back. We lose our patience. We snap at the wrong moment. We forget to follow through on something we promised. We get distracted, overwhelmed, or caught up in our own stress, and we misread the room. Sometimes we hurt someone without even realizing it until later. Not because we're careless or cruel, but because we're human. Imperfect, emotional, and still learning.

Mistakes are unavoidable.

They come with relationships, with responsibilities, and with simply moving through the world. But the important part is not whether you make mistakes, because you will. The real question is what you do next. Do you take ownership, or do you deflect? Do you acknowledge your part, or do you pretend it did not happen? That is where character shows up. Responsibility is what separates someone who grows from their mistakes from someone who just keeps repeating them. Owning your impact is where repair begins.

And responsibility starts with five words: "I'm sorry. I was wrong."

The apology doesn't need to be elaborate. You don't need to explain for ten minutes. You don't need to turn the apology into a defense of your behavior or a list of excuses. Just own it. Keep it simple. Be clear. And be sincere.

Think about a time someone hurt you. It might have been small from the outside, but it stayed with you. Maybe a friend did not show up when you needed them. Maybe someone dismissed your feelings or said something that cut deeper than they realized. It could have been a broken promise or just a silence that came when you expected support.

In that moment, you did not need them to be perfect. You did not need a big performance. What you wanted most was acknowledgment. Something honest. Something human. A simple apology would have meant everything.

Now turn it around. Think of a time when you were the one who hurt someone. Maybe you didn't mean to. Maybe it took time to realize it. But something told you that you played a part in their pain. And maybe you didn't say anything. Maybe you hoped it would blow over. Maybe you waited so long it felt awkward to bring it up again.

But somewhere inside, you knew you left something unfinished. That is the part we all wrestle with. We want to move forward, but we avoid the one thing that can actually help us do it. Saying sorry. Not because it erases the past, but because it takes ownership of it.

That's where healing begins.

But here's the thing. A late apology is still better than none. Even if time has passed. Even if things feel awkward. Even if the other person never brings it up again. A genuine apology still holds power. It's a moment of honesty that clears the air. That says, "I see what I did. And I need to own it."

Apologizing doesn't erase the mistake.

But it does show growth. It shows maturity. It tells the other person that their feelings matter. It tells them you're not afraid to look at yourself honestly. That builds trust. That rebuilds connection.

And it's not just about big, dramatic moments. Apologies matter in the small, everyday ones too. Interrupting someone. Dismissing their idea. Speaking sharply when you're stressed. Forgetting to follow through. All of those moments deserve acknowledgment. The little hurts add up. And the little apologies help soften them.

Some people think that saying sorry too often makes you seem unsure of yourself. But that is only true if the apology is used as a reflex, not a reflection. There is a difference between saying "sorry" when you are not wrong, and saying it when you are. One is insecurity. The other is integrity.

A strong apology does not shrink you.

It does not take away from your dignity, your intelligence, or your credibility. It anchors you. It shows that you are strong enough to look at yourself honestly, and secure enough to admit when you have caused harm.

It doesn't say you have all the answers. It doesn't pretend you handled everything perfectly. It simply says, "I know who I am. I am not perfect. But I am accountable." That kind of self-awareness is powerful. It builds trust. It creates space for healing. It tells the people around you they don't have to walk on eggshells. They see that you are capable of owning your actions and growing from them.

And if you're worried about being taken advantage of, remember this: apologizing isn't the same as surrendering. It doesn't mean you're admitting to everything or taking on blame that isn't yours. Don't confuse accountability with self-blame.

A sincere apology is not about giving up your voice. It is about using it responsibly. You can own your part without carrying someone else's.

You can say, "I was wrong to raise my voice," without adding, "and everything is my fault."

You can acknowledge the way you showed up in a moment without absorbing the entire weight of what went wrong. A healthy apology is focused. It is clear. It doesn't overreach. It doesn't collapse under guilt. It simply names the thing you're responsible for and leaves the rest where it belongs.

Owning your part means exactly that, your part. Not more and not less. It is an act of strength, not submission. And it sets a boundary at the same time it opens a door.

This kind of self-awareness shows up everywhere. In personal relationships. In families. In leadership. The best leaders aren't the ones who never mess up. They're the ones who admit when they do, and work to fix it. That creates safety. It creates respect. People are far more willing to follow someone who takes responsibility than someone who hides behind pride.

There is something freeing about apologizing. It is for you as much as for the other person.

Guilt and regret are heavy burdens. They sit quietly in your mind, pressing on you when you're alone. You replay what you said, wonder how it came across, and think about what you should have done differently. You feel the shift in the relationship. There is less closeness and more tension. You pretend it isn't there, but you notice it every time you talk.

You start to avoid the conversation, not because you don't care, but because it feels uncomfortable. And the longer it goes unspoken, the more awkward it feels to bring it up. So the silence stays. And the distance grows.

But when you apologize, you release that weight. You stop carrying the moment like a secret. You let it breathe. You open the door to repair, even if the other person is not ready to walk through it yet. You give both of you a way forward. You replace guessing with honesty. And sometimes, that alone is enough to restore peace, both in the relationship and within yourself.

So if you need to say sorry, say it.

Say it plainly. Say it without conditions. Say it because it's the right thing to do.

Then show it.

Apologizing is step one.

Changing the behavior is step two.

If you hurt someone and then keep doing the same thing, the apology becomes empty. But when you back it up with action, it becomes real. It becomes a turning point.

And don't underestimate what it can do. A simple apology can repair a relationship. It can ease tension. It can soften someone's heart. It can make room for healing.

That is not weakness.

That is strength.

That is common sense.

Never Burn Bridges Unless You're Absolutely Sure

It can feel satisfying to make a dramatic exit. To slam the door behind you, even if only in your mind, and think, *That's it. I am done.* There is a rush in that moment. A feeling of finality. Of drawing a bold line and declaring you will not be crossed again.

It feels like taking your power back. Like standing up for yourself in a world that often tells you to stay quiet. You tell yourself you are done being taken for granted. That you have learned your lesson. That you don't need them. That you have outgrown the situation. That moving on without looking back is the strong thing to do.

And sometimes you are right. Walking away can be the healthiest choice.

There are moments when staying would cost more than leaving. When you have done the work, thought it through, and know deep down that this door needs to close. Some bridges were never built on solid ground in the first place. Letting them go can be a form of healing.

But what matters most is not that you walked away. It is how you did it. Sometimes burning the bridge causes more damage than the original problem ever did.

What starts as a moment of frustration or a burst of anger can turn into something lasting. Not just for the other person, but for you.

Cutting someone off completely, especially in the heat of the moment, often leaves something behind. A heaviness. A sense that things were left unfinished. You carry it longer than you thought you would. You replay how it ended. You wonder if it had to go that way.

Once the bridge is gone, it's not easy to rebuild. The path back is overgrown with silence, pride, and the weight of everything that was left unsaid.

That's why it is worth pausing before you light the match. Not every exit needs to be a firestorm. Not every goodbye has to scorch the ground behind it. There is a difference between setting a boundary and setting fire to the connection. Setting a boundary means protecting your peace. Burning a bridge means making sure there is no way back, even if one day you might want one.

Walking away doesn't always mean you have to erase the path behind you.

Sometimes the wisest thing you can do is leave the door cracked. Not because you expect to walk through it again, but because you know that life is unpredictable. People grow. Circumstances change. The story you are living right now is not the whole story.

What feels clear today might look different in a year, or in five, or in ten. Leaving room for that possibility is not a sign of weakness. It is a sign of maturity. It means you can protect yourself without becoming hard. It means you can choose peace over permanence, and still move forward with clarity.

Think about how small the world can be. It is easy to forget, especially when you are caught in the emotions of a moment, how often paths cross again.

A former coworker you barely spoke to becomes a hiring manager at a company you want to work for. An old classmate you have not thought about in years shows up as a connection at a networking event. Someone you had a falling-out with, someone you thought was gone from your life, ends up sitting across from you at a meeting, or at the same dinner table through mutual friends. It happens more than people realize.

And when it does, the way you ended things becomes the loudest part of the memory. Not the good moments. Not the shared history. The exit. That is what sticks.

Did you leave things respectfully? Or did you let them explode? Did you say what needed to be said with clarity and calm? Or did you burn the whole thing down because it felt good in the moment?

When your name comes up later, and it will, how that last moment felt may be the thing people remember most. Sometimes you don't get to offer a new version of yourself. You only get the legacy of how you handled goodbye.

That's why it matters. Not because you need to stay connected to everyone forever, but because parting ways with grace is a quiet kind of power. It tells the world who you are, even when no one is watching.

We've all had situations where the urge to burn the bridge was strong. Maybe it was a job that made you feel undervalued. Maybe it was a friendship that became one-sided. Maybe it was a conversation that turned into a fight. And maybe, in that moment, it felt like you had every right to walk away without looking back.

But here's what people forget. There's a way to leave without destroying everything behind you. You can step away without bitterness. You can express what hurt you without insulting the other person. You can say goodbye without making it a performance. It doesn't have to be a dramatic final scene. It can be quiet. Firm. Respectful.

And that respect, even when it's not returned, says a lot about you.

This doesn't mean you have to keep everyone in your life forever.

Some relationships do need to end. Some jobs are not worth staying in. Some environments are not healthy to return to. But there's a big difference between closing a chapter and tearing out the page. One leaves room for peace. The other leaves ash.

Ask yourself a simple question. If I saw this person again in five years, how would I want to feel? Would I want to look the other way, hoping they didn't notice me? Would I want to pretend we never knew each other, shrinking from the memory of how it all ended? Or would I rather be able to nod, smile politely, and move forward with ease? Would I rather be able to say, even just silently, that I handled myself with maturity? That I didn't let anger, ego, or pride dictate my last impression?

That answer can shape how you leave. It can remind you that the final chapter doesn't have to be loud to be strong. It can be quiet. Clean. Clear.

You don't need to make a speech or prove a point. You only need to ask yourself how you will feel later, not just right now, but months or years from now when the emotion has faded and only the memory remains.

Because the truth is, burning bridges rarely gives you as much lasting satisfaction as it promises in the moment. Sure, it can feel like release. A sense of closure. A moment of *At least I got it off my chest*. But more often than not, that high is short-lived. It fades, and something else takes its place. Reflection. Doubt. Regret.

You start to wonder if you could have handled it differently. If you could have said less, or said it more kindly. If you could have made your exit without making it final. That kind of regret doesn't always come with dramatic consequences. But it lingers. It adds weight to your story. And it leaves you wondering what might have happened if you had paused, breathed, and chosen a softer landing.

You don't have to be friends with everyone.

You don't have to explain yourself endlessly. You don't have to fake closeness that no longer feels real. But you can leave people with dignity. You can exit quietly and still with strength. And you can hold your boundaries without destroying the whole road behind you.

The world is unpredictable.

People grow. Circumstances change. And sometimes, people who once hurt you do the work to become better. Sometimes they come back. Sometimes you do. Sometimes things come full circle in ways you couldn't have imagined.

And when that happens, you'll be glad you didn't burn it all down.

Keep your distance when you need to. Stand up for yourself. Make the choices that protect your peace.

But leave the bridge standing if you can.

You never know when you might need to cross it again.

That is not giving in.

That is being thoughtful.

That is common sense.

Don't Try to Win Arguments. Try to Solve Problems.

It is easy to get pulled into the idea of winning. Proving a point. Showing that the other person was wrong. Walking away from a discussion with the satisfaction of knowing you came out on top.

But winning an argument is not the same as fixing the problem.

You can win the debate and still leave the real issue untouched. You can score verbal points and still go home with tension in the air. You can have the sharper comebacks and still wake up to the same problem waiting for you in the morning.

When the goal is to win, the focus changes. It is no longer about the issue. It is about the scoreboard.

It becomes about defending a position, even if holding it makes the situation worse. Pride takes the wheel. The focus shifts to protecting the argument rather than improving the situation. Every word is chosen to score a point, to counter, to prove. Not to understand.

When the goal is to solve the problem, the tone changes. The conversation slows. The heat comes down. There is room to actually hear the other person instead of simply waiting for a turn to speak. Questions replace accusations. Curiosity replaces combat. The goal becomes finding common ground and moving toward a better outcome. Not one person standing over the other, but both walking away having gained something.

In most arguments, both sides believe they are right.

Each is convinced they see the truth clearly. If the only goal is to win, the argument goes in circles until one person gets tired, changes the subject, or walks away. Nothing is learned. Nothing changes.

But if the goal is to solve the problem, there is a shift. There is curiosity. There are questions like, "What do you need from this?" or "What would make this better for both of us?"

There is a search for common ground, not just for cracks in the other person's case.

It does not mean surrendering or giving in just to keep the peace. It is not about silencing yourself or pretending the issue does not matter.

It means aiming for a result that changes something for the better. A result that removes the frustration or confusion that started the conflict in the first place. A result that makes the next conversation easier, not harder. It is about creating progress instead of collecting points. About fixing what is wrong instead of proving who was right.

Picture two co-workers arguing about how to handle a project deadline. One insists that the only solution is to push harder, work longer hours, and finish on time no matter what. The other says the deadline is unrealistic and that rushing will cause the quality to suffer.

If the goal is to win, each one digs in. They repeat their own point louder, looking for ways to discredit the other. Flaws in past work get dragged into the conversation. Old mistakes are brought up as proof. Energy shifts away from the project and toward defending personal pride. The discussion becomes about who is right rather than what will work.

If the goal is to solve the problem, the tone shifts. The conversation opens. They start exploring possibilities. Could the deadline be adjusted without derailing the bigger plan? Could extra resources be brought in to help meet it? Could the work be split into phases so progress is made without sacrificing quality? Instead of defending themselves, they defend the outcome. The focus returns to the work, not the battle.

Or picture a couple arguing about chores. One feels overworked and says they are carrying more than their share. The other feels unappreciated and says they are doing just as much. Both are tired. Both believe they are right.

But the goal is not to win. The goal is to understand and solve the problem.

If the goal is to win, the evening turns into a scoreboard. Each starts tallying every dish washed, every floor swept, every bag of garbage taken out. They point out the times the other forgot to do something. They hold on to small grievances as if they were proof in a trial. By the end, nothing feels resolved, except that both are more frustrated than when they began.

If the goal is to solve the problem, the tone changes.

It stops being about blame and starts being about balance. They begin to ask, "How can we split this in a way that feels fair?" or "What would make this easier for both of us?" Instead of listing old chores, they talk about the ones ahead. The argument becomes a plan. And the energy that would have gone into winning is used to build something they can both agree on.

Even small everyday disagreements work the same way. Two friends cannot agree on where to eat. One wants pizza. The other wants sushi.

If the goal is to win, they keep repeating why their choice is better until someone finally gives in with a sigh.

If the goal is to solve the problem, they might find a place that serves both, or agree to get pizza this time and sushi next time. No one "wins," but no one loses either.

Winning can feel good in the moment, but it comes with a cost.

People remember how they felt during the argument long after they forget who "won" it. If someone feels dismissed, humiliated, or unheard, the relationship doesn't stay the same. It gets quieter. Colder. Less trusting.

And the next disagreement doesn't start from a clean slate.

It starts with leftover tension. With defensiveness already in the air. With both people a little less willing to listen. The tone is colder. The patience is thinner.

Small misunderstandings feel bigger than they are because they pile up on unresolved issues. With both people a little less willing to listen.

Focusing on solving the problem changes that pattern. It builds trust instead of eroding it. It sends the message, "We are on the same side, even if we see things differently." That mindset makes the next conversation easier, not harder.

Sometimes this means stepping back and asking, "What is the real issue here?" Arguments often start about one thing but are fueled by something deeper.

A fight about where to spend the weekend might really be about feeling ignored. A disagreement about money might really be about feeling unsafe. Solving the problem means finding and addressing that deeper layer, not just the surface argument.

It also means letting go of the need to have the last word. The last word feels powerful, but it often does nothing to move things forward. In fact, it can be the thing that shuts down a chance to fix the problem.

And yes, it might mean admitting when the other person has a point. That doesn't make you weaker. It makes you credible. It shows that the truth matters more than your ego.

Shifting from winning to solving is like changing from a game of tug-of-war to building something together. In tug-of-war, every gain for one side is a loss for the other. In building, every step forward makes the structure stronger for both.

Solving problems also leaves fewer loose ends. Arguments fought just to be won tend to pop back up later, often in disguise. But when the focus is on fixing the root cause, the same problem doesn't need to be fought over again.

It is not always neat or quick. Real solutions take patience. They take a willingness to slow down and see the bigger picture.

But they are worth it.

In the end, the scoreboard does not matter if the problem stays unsolved.

What matters is leaving the conversation in a better place than where it began.

Focus on solving the problem, not winning the argument.

That is the win that lasts.

That is common sense.

Surround Yourself with People Who Make You Better

The company you keep shapes your life. The people closest to you influence your mood, your pace, your goals, and your standards. Some pull you forward. Some hold you in place. Some drain you without even trying. Pay attention to how you feel after being with them. Do you leave lighter or heavier? Clearer or foggier? That is your clue.

The impact is real, even when it's subtle.

That is why who you choose to be around matters. Not just the people you happen to work with or the ones you have known the longest. The people who are closest to you set the pace you run at.

Choose people who want good things for you and tell you the truth. People who celebrate your wins without keeping score. People who challenge you without tearing you down. The more of that you have around you, the easier for you to keep growing.

It is easy to hold on to certain relationships out of habit. Maybe you have known them since high school. Maybe you used to be close. Maybe you still see them every weekend or check in because it feels like the right thing to do. There is history there. Familiar rhythms. A sense of comfort in what is known. And sometimes that comfort is what keeps you showing up, even when the relationship no longer adds anything meaningful to your life.

But familiarity is not the same as growth.

Just because someone has been in your life a long time doesn't mean they are still good for you. Sometimes you are holding on to a version of the relationship that no longer exists. You keep showing up out of habit, not connection. You cling to a dynamic that once worked but now leaves you feeling drained, confused, or stuck.

Being around someone all the time doesn't mean they are helping you move forward. It just means they are part of your routine. Like a habit you never stopped to question. And sometimes, routines need to change. Sometimes you change. And if the people around you are not growing with you, it's worth asking whether the relationship is still serving either of you.

That is not selfish. That is clarity.

Start paying attention to how you feel after spending time with someone. Do you feel lighter? Calmer? More focused? More confident in who you are? Or do you feel tense? Insecure? Judged? Drained? Your body often knows before your mind catches up. If someone leaves you feeling worse more often than better, that is worth noticing.

The right people bring out your best without making you feel like you are not enough. They challenge you to grow, to be honest with yourself, and to take ownership of your choices. But they never do it in a way that tears you down. Instead of pointing fingers, they hold up a mirror. Their feedback is rooted in care, not criticism, and it comes from a place of wanting to see you thrive.

You can trust them to hold you accountable while still making you feel supported. They will speak up when you are off track, but they do it gently, without judgment. They remind you of who you are when you forget. On days when you feel small or uncertain, they speak to your potential. Not with pressure, but with belief. Their presence helps you return to yourself.

And when life shifts, when you are celebrating a win or navigating a loss, they do not disappear. They show up fully. They cheer for your victories with genuine joy and stay close through your setbacks without needing to fix them.

What they offer is not performance, but loyalty. Not convenience, but commitment. They want to see you do well, not because it helps them, but because they simply care.

And when you find people like that, you hold on. You make space for them. And you try to be that kind of person in return.

You don't need perfect friends.

No one gets everything right. You do not need the most successful, impressive, or well-connected people around you. You don't need a circle of people that looks good on paper. What you need are people who bring out your better side. Not by pushing you constantly, but by showing up in ways that help you rise.

You need people who tell you the truth when it matters. Not just when it's easy. Not just when it sounds good. People who care enough to be honest, even if it makes things uncomfortable.

You need people who are growing, too. People who are doing the work to become more self-aware, more thoughtful, more genuine Not perfect. Just intentional. Because people who are growing do not get defensive when you grow too. They do not shrink in your light. They do not make your progress feel like a problem. They encourage it. They support it. And they walk their own path alongside yours, not in competition, but in quiet companionship.

This kind of circle may not be large. It may not be loud. But it will feel real. And over time, that matters far more than anything else.

Think about the people in your life who inspire you.

They may not be loud or flashy. But something about the way they live makes you want to be more thoughtful, more disciplined, more generous, more powerful. That is no accident. Being around someone who lives with purpose makes it easier for you to do the same.

On the other hand, you also know what it feels like to be pulled down. Maybe it's the friend who always complains but never takes action. Or the coworker who gossips and gets defensive when you do not join in. Or the person who jokes at your expense and calls it "just teasing." Over time, these dynamics chip away at your self-respect. They make you second-guess yourself. They keep you playing small, because stepping into your full self would make them uncomfortable.

It is not selfish to step back from that. It is smart.

You cannot become who you are meant to be while constantly managing other people's insecurities. You cannot rise while being dragged by those who prefer you stuck.

This does not mean cutting everyone off the second they annoy you. People are human. They are going to mess up, and so are you. The goal is not to build a flawless circle. The goal is to build a real one. One where there is trust. Where you can be honest. Where growth is mutual, not one-sided.

Sometimes, that means outgrowing certain relationships. Sometimes, it means having hard conversations. Sometimes, it means letting go of someone who has been in your life for years, not because they are a bad person, but because the dynamic no longer serves either of you.

Other times, it means putting in the work to deepen the relationships that are already good. Checking in more often. Showing up more consistently. Being the kind of friend you want to have. Because building a circle that lifts you up is not just about what others give. It is also about what you bring to the table.

You become like the people you are around most.

That happens slowly, almost without realizing it. Their language starts to become your language. Their habits influence your own. The way they think, the way they react, the way they talk about others, it all starts to seep into your day-to-day life.

Their energy becomes part of your environment. If they are negative, you feel heavier. If they are driven, you start to think bigger. If they gossip, you find yourself pulled into it. If they take ownership of their lives, you begin to reflect on your own with more clarity.

It is not about imitation. It is about atmosphere. Just like spending time in a cluttered room affects how you feel, spending time with people who are scattered, bitter, or stuck can do the same. And the opposite is true, too. When you surround yourself with people who are kind, thoughtful, motivated, and real, it becomes easier to show up that way yourself. You start to level up without even trying to compete, simply because being around them makes you want to do better.

Whether you mean it to or not, who you are around will shape who you become. That is why being intentional about your circle is not selfish. It is necessary.

So, choose wisely.

Choose people who make you think, who make you laugh, who make you want to grow. People who challenge you in the right ways. Who speak to your potential, not just your past. Who hold you steady when life shakes, and celebrate your wins without making them about themselves.

With people like that, you do not just feel supported.

You keep learning.

You keep growing.

You become a better version of yourself simply by being around them.

That is common sense.

Treat People Better Than They Treat You (But Don't Be a Doormat)

It is easy to treat people well when they treat you well first. When they're kind. When they listen. When they respond with patience and grace. That's not hard. It feels natural. Almost automatic. You smile because they smiled. You are patient because they were. You meet their respect with your own, and the whole thing runs smoothly. It feels balanced, effortless.

But that's not the part that shows who you really are.

The real test comes when someone makes it difficult. When they cut you off mid-sentence. When they roll their eyes. When they forget to say thank you or choose not to show up at all.

It's in those moments, when someone else drops the standard, that your own values step in. Do you match their energy? Do you snap back? Do you take the bait? Or do you stay steady, not because they deserve it, but because you've already decided who you are going to be?

That's where it counts. Not when it's easy. But when it's not.

You don't have to match someone's bad behavior to prove a point.

Just because they were rude doesn't mean you need to be. Just because they made a jab doesn't mean you need to return it. You can notice someone's attitude and still decide not to carry it with you. You can hold your ground without sinking to their level.

Responding with the same energy might feel satisfying for a second, but it rarely leads anywhere good. It turns a moment into a mess.

There is nothing impressive about meeting disrespect with more disrespect. That is not strength. That is just reaction.

Real strength is choosing a better response when it would be easier not to.

The strongest people are not the ones who win every argument or shut others down. They are the ones who stay grounded. Who remember their values even when the moment would justify forgetting them. They do not get dragged into every storm that passes. They pause. They decide. And then they respond with strength.

Choosing respect when it is not handed to you doesn't mean you are letting it slide. It doesn't mean you missed the shift in tone. It doesn't mean you are blind to the passive aggression, the subtle digs, or the way someone tried to rattle you. You noticed. You felt it. You simply chose not to let it define your next move.

It means you are not giving them the satisfaction of pulling you out of character. You are not handing over your peace just because someone else lost theirs. You are not going to mirror bad behavior just to feel powerful for a moment.

That kind of control comes from steadiness, not from shouting or showing off.

You don't need to shout to be taken seriously. You don't need to prove your strength through volume or reaction. Some things are not worth the energy it takes to fight them. Some things are better answered with calm presence, with the kind of self-control that speaks louder than any comeback.

But let's be clear. Respecting someone doesn't mean staying silent when something crosses a line. Being kind doesn't mean being quiet forever. It doesn't mean allowing the same behavior again and again just to avoid tension.

There's a difference between being patient and being passive. There's a difference between giving someone grace and giving them your peace of mind. One helps the relationship grow. The other slowly wears you down.

You can forgive someone and still recognize that the relationship has changed. You can wish someone well and still decide they don't need a front-row seat in your life. You can treat someone decently, not because they earned it, but because you've decided to lead with character, and still set boundaries. That's not cruel. That's clarity. And that's what allows kindness to be real instead of wearing you down. You're not abandoning people. You're refusing to abandon yourself.

Being kind doesn't mean you keep the peace at your own expense. It doesn't mean biting your tongue until you're resentful. It doesn't mean swallowing your feelings so someone else can stay comfortable. When kindness turns into self-abandonment, it stops being kindness. It becomes something else, something that slowly wears you down.

Avoiding conflict might feel easier in the moment. It keeps things smooth. It avoids discomfort. It gives you the illusion of peace. But underneath that temporary ease, something starts to build. Tension. Frustration. Quiet resentment. You tell yourself it's not worth the fight. You convince yourself to let it go. You smile. You nod. You carry on like nothing is wrong.

But something is.

Over time, you start to feel overlooked. Unheard. Taken for granted. You notice the patterns. The subtle dismissals. The small ways your needs or feelings keep getting pushed aside. And the worst part is that most people will not even realize it's happening. Because you never told them. You never pushed back. You never showed them where the line was.

You said it was fine. You laughed it off. You held your breath to keep the peace.

But inside, a crack begins to form.

Not out of rage. Not out of bitterness. Out of fatigue.

The fatigue of carrying too much without asking for help. Of tolerating things that quietly drain you. Of shrinking to make space for other people's comfort while ignoring your own. And eventually, that quiet fatigue turns into distance. You start pulling back. You care a little less. You engage a little less. You show up, but not fully. Because part of you is tired of pretending it doesn't hurt.

Real kindness doesn't require you to perform. It doesn't ask you to play small. It knows when to speak and when to walk away. It sets limits, not as punishment, but as protection. It doesn't come from a need to be liked. It comes from knowing your worth.

And once you know that, you stop begging for the bare minimum. You stop explaining your value to people who can't see it.

True kindness sounds like, "I care about you, but I'm not going to keep sacrificing my peace to prove it." It sounds like, "I'm here, but I won't stay in something that keeps hurting." It sounds like, "I wish you well, but I need something healthier for myself." And sometimes it sounds like silence. A silence that says, "I'm done talking. I'm making a change."

People may mistake your patience for weakness.

They may think your calm means you didn't care. They may assume that because you didn't react, you didn't notice. But there's a big difference between being unaware and being intentional. Sometimes you see everything. You just choose not to respond in a way that adds more noise. And that decision? That's power.

You're not here to win every argument or clap back at every offense.

You're not here to convince people that you're right.

You're here to live in a way that lets you respect. Because the truth is, the words you don't say, the ones you hold back because they won't help, often reveal more strength than the ones you do. Silence can power, not surrender.

That kind of strength doesn't shout. It doesn't need to. It knows what matters and what doesn't. It knows when to stay silent and when to speak with purpose. It knows that real control isn't about dominating the moment. It's about not letting the moment control you.

Moving on is not always giving up. Sometimes it is choosing to rise above, without drama or noise. It is a quiet decision, made with clarity. You leave, not because you are weak, but because you are ready to protect your peace. You walk away with your self-respect intact and your energy no longer scattered.

So yes, treat people better than they treat you. Choose to be someone who lives with intention, not reaction. Someone who can be gentle and still be firm. Someone who doesn't take the low road, even when it's wide open.

Being the bigger person doesn't mean disappearing. It doesn't mean letting people treat you badly just to keep the peace. If you are always ignoring your feelings, always staying quiet, always putting others first no matter the cost, you are not rising above. You are fading out. Kindness needs limits. You can be gentle without being walked on. You can forgive without pretending it didn't hurt. Choosing peace should not mean losing yourself.

You're allowed to expect better.

You're allowed to leave.

You're allowed to stop giving second chances when someone keeps giving you the same hurt.

Choose kindness, but carry a backbone.

That is not just emotional maturity.

That is common sense.

PART FOUR

Tools for Life

Tools for Life

You cannot avoid every problem, but you can be ready. Life is not easy, yet the right tools prepare you. Clear words stop small conflicts from becoming big ones. Reflection turns mistakes into lessons. Action, even when you are unsure, keeps you moving forward. None of this is magic. These are simple habits that make you steadier, calmer, and more resourceful.

Learn How to Cook a Few Meals Well

Let's get something straight right away. You don't have to be a chef. You don't need a signature sauce or a collection of expensive knives or a deep knowledge of French culinary terms. No one is asking you to become the next Gordon Ramsay.

But you should learn how to cook a few meals. Really cook them. Not just warm something up. Not just survive. Cook. Well.

Because cooking isn't just about food. It is about self-respect. It is about taking care of yourself in a way that says, *I'm not waiting around for someone else to do this for me.* It is about knowing that no matter what's going on in your life, money, stress, chaos, you can still feed yourself a good meal. One you made with your own hands.

It is one of the simplest things that makes life feel more manageable.

And for some reason, we treat it like an optional skill. Something you learn only if you're "into that kind of thing." As if cooking is some quirky side hobby, not a basic life skill. As if it's only for people who get excited about recipes or have the right cookware or grew up watching cooking shows.

We act like it's extra credit. A bonus. Something you can do if you feel like it, but not something that really matters. Something that's nice to know, but not essential. As if feeding yourself isn't a core part of being a functioning human being.

But it is. It absolutely is.

Feeding yourself is not optional. Cooking is not extra. It is not a niche interest or something reserved for people who happen to enjoy it. It is basic. It is necessary. It is part of taking care of yourself in the most practical way.

You need food. Your body needs food.

That means someone has to make it.

And that someone, at least some of the time, should be you. Not a restaurant. Not a frozen box. Not a delivery app. You. That's not about being impressive. It is about being responsible. It is about knowing that when all else fails, when money is tight, when life is chaotic, when options are limited, you can still feed yourself. You can still take care of yourself. You can still meet that basic need without falling apart. And that matters.

Knowing how to cook a few meals well gives you freedom. It means you are not stuck eating whatever is fast, cheap, or microwavable. It means you are not dependent on takeout, someone else's schedule, or a sad vending machine at the end of a long day. It means that even when the rest of your life feels messy, you can still stand over a stove, stir a pot, and say, "I got this."

And here's the truth: cooking is not as complicated as people make it seem.

You don't need to memorize a cookbook. You don't need to buy a dozen spices you'll never touch again. You just need a few basics. A few solid meals you can make without Googling every step. Meals you can rely on. Meals that taste good. Meals that feel like care. Even if you're only making them for yourself.

You need a go-to breakfast that's more than cereal. A simple dinner you can whip up after a long day. Something you can serve to a guest without apologizing. A meal that feels like comfort. A meal that feels like confidence.

Start there.

Learn how to make scrambled eggs, really good ones. Learn how to roast vegetables until they are caramelized and golden, not soggy and sad. Learn how to make pasta that isn't drowning in sauce. Learn how to grill a piece of meat or cook tofu that actually tastes like something. Learn how to chop an onion without crying (too much).

Pick a handful of meals. Practice them. Make them so many times that the steps live in your body. That you don't need to measure every ingredient to get it right. That you don't need a recipe. You just need ingredients and a bit of rhythm.

Because cooking is rhythm. It is presence. It is pacing. It is patience.

Here's the secret: most people who cook "well" aren't doing anything fancy. They're not relying on complicated techniques or exotic ingredients. They've just made the same meals enough times to know the steps by heart. They've burned a few things. They've overcooked, under-seasoned, and learned from it. Over time, cooking has become part of their DNA. They know when to stir, when to wait, and when to turn the heat down.

They move with confidence, and that confidence shows in the result. Not because the ingredients are any different, but because the process is smoother. The timing is better. The mistakes are fewer. They're not second-guessing every step, and that makes a difference in how the food turns out. It is not about being perfect. It is about being capable.

It is not about being perfect. It is not about flawless execution or picture-worthy plates. It is about being capable. Being steady. Being able to walk into your kitchen, grab what you need, and make something real without panic. That's the kind of skill that sticks.

Because when you know how to cook, your life changes in small but powerful ways.

You stop skipping meals. You stop spending money you don't have. You stop feeling helpless when it's time to eat and the fridge looks empty. You start inviting people over. You start experimenting. You start building a little ritual into your day. You start feeling like you have more control. Not over everything, but over something.

And that matters.

Cooking is not just about food. It is about taking charge of your life in a small but meaningful way. It is about care. It is about the simple, steady act of saying: *I can take care of myself. I can make something from nothing. I can create something nourishing.*

Even if the rest of the day felt like a mess, a good meal reminds you there is still something you can control.

And the thing is, you don't need to do it every night. You just need to be able to do it when it counts.

When money is tight. When you're trying to eat better. When you're cooking for someone you care about. When you're feeling low and just want something warm. When you've had a bad day and need a win. When you want to feel human again.

A well-cooked meal can do that. Especially when you made it.

And yes, you'll mess up. You'll burn things. You'll forget the salt. You'll drop food on the floor. That's part of it. That's how you learn. Every great cook started with a few disasters.

But the more you try, the more you learn. And the more you learn, the more it feels like second nature.

You'll start to feel the heat of the pan instead of checking a timer. You'll start to taste things and know exactly what's missing. You'll start to feel the rhythm of cooking. The chopping, the stirring, the sizzling. And it will feel less like following instructions and more like knowing what comes next. It will feel like presence.

That's what cooking can give you: presence. In a world that's always rushing, always distracted, always outsourcing the basics, cooking brings you back to earth. It grounds you. It slows you down. It reminds you to take care of yourself in the most literal way.

So don't wait until life forces you to learn. Don't wait until you're broke, or sick, or suddenly on your own. Don't wait until the last minute to figure out how to boil water. Start now. Learn now.

Start with something small. One meal. One recipe. One moment in the kitchen. Burn it. Fix it. Try again.

It is not only about what ends up on the plate.

It is about building a simple, steady skill that says, *I've got this. I can handle things. I can take care of myself. I can turn ingredients into something real.*

This is not just about food. It is about reminding yourself that you are capable, resourceful, and enough.

That is something that matters.

That is common sense.

Learn Basic First Aid

Here's something most people don't think about until it's too late: you should know some basic first aid. You should know what to do in an emergency, even if it's just the simple stuff. A few small actions can make a big difference when it counts.

Not the big dramatic ones from movies. Just the regular, real-life stuff. Someone slices their hand in the kitchen. A kid takes a bad fall on the sidewalk. A friend burns their arm on the oven. A stranger starts choking in a restaurant. These things happen. More often than you'd expect.

Sometimes, it's even more serious. Someone collapses without warning. They stop breathing. Their heart stops. They go into shock. There's no time to wait, no time to guess. What happens in the next few seconds can mean everything. In those moments, the difference between panic and action is usually just one thing.

A person who knows CPR can keep blood flowing to the brain. A person who knows how to use an EpiPen can stop a severe allergic reaction. A person who stays calm can stop bleeding or clear a blocked airway.

These aren't just helpful skills. They are life-saving actions. And they don't take much to learn.

Someone in the room should know what to do.

That someone can be you.

You don't need a degree. You don't need special gear. You don't need to be fearless or strong or even all that confident. You just need to know the basics. You need to have taken a little time, once, when nothing was wrong, to learn what to do when something goes wrong.

Because when something actually does go wrong, you won't have time to Google it.

You won't have time to scroll through articles, look for a video, or read instructions. You'll need to act. Quickly. Calmly. Clearly. And the only way that happens is if you already know what to do.

This is one of those skills that gives you quiet power. It is not loud. It does not draw attention. You don't talk about it much, and most days, you don't even think about it. It just stays in the background of your life, steady and unnoticed.

But when something goes wrong, when someone gets hurt or collapses or cannot breathe, that quiet skill becomes the most important thing in the room. In an instant, everything changes. The person who knows what to do becomes the one everyone is looking to.

And it's not hard to learn.

In a couple of hours, you can learn how to treat a deep cut. How to clean a wound. How to cool a burn. How to use an EpiPen. How to recognize the signs of a stroke. How to do CPR. How to help someone who's choking. How to support a person in shock. None of it is complicated. Most of it is just being prepared and staying calm. But it can make the difference between a full recovery and a tragedy.

It is not about becoming a hero.

It is not about charging in and taking over. Most of the time, it's the opposite. It is about staying calm while everyone else is panicking. It is about keeping your voice steady. It is about saying to yourself, *I know what to do. I'm here.* That presence can change everything.

Because in emergencies, people don't just need treatment. They need someone who isn't falling apart.

And that can be you. Not because you are fearless, but because you are prepared.

Learning basic first aid is a way of saying, *I am not waiting until something goes wrong to get ready. I am not going to leave it to chance or hope that someone else knows what to do. I am going to build this skill now, quietly and without fanfare, without waiting for a close call to wake me up. I am going to prepare while things are calm, so that if the moment ever comes and someone needs help, I am not scrambling or guessing. I am not panicking. I am stepping in. I am ready to act.*

And just like with anything else, practice matters.

It is one thing to know the steps. It is another to have gone through them. Take a first aid course if you can. Go through a CPR demo. Watch a real-time video and follow along. Try using a bandage properly. Walk yourself through a scenario. Even a little hands-on practice makes a big difference in how you'll respond under pressure.

And if you forget the details later, fine. You'll still be more prepared than if you'd never learned at all.

The goal is not perfection.

You do not need to perform every step flawlessly or remember every detail under pressure.

The goal is not memorizing every medical term or acting like a professional. The goal is simply being useful. Being present. Being the kind of person who doesn't freeze when something goes wrong. Someone who stays steady. Someone who knows what to do, even if it's just the basics. Someone who can step forward and offer help, even if it's just keeping someone calm or applying pressure to a wound. Even a small action, done with care, can make a very big difference.

And the truth is, the world needs more people like that.

Learn Basic First Aid

We spend so much time learning things we might never use, like obscure math formulas, historical trivia, and random school facts. Yet many of us have no idea what to do if someone has a seizure at the bus stop. Or if a child chokes at dinner. Or if a coworker faints in front of us.

It is not because we're lazy. It is because no one ever insisted this was important.

But it is.

It is very important. Not flashy. Not exciting. But essential. And it's so easy to learn. You can spend one afternoon watching a few trusted tutorials. One evening reading a guide from a reliable source. A weekend morning in a community first aid class. That's all it takes.

And most people won't do it. That's just the truth.

But you can.

And once you do, you'll carry that skill quietly. You won't talk about it much. You won't think about it often. But one day, maybe years from now, someone near you will need help. And while everyone else freezes or backs away, you'll step forward. Not because you're the expert, but because you're the one who bothered to learn.

That's what real preparation looks like. It is not about living in fear or expecting disaster around every corner. It is not about being paranoid or imagining the worst at all times. It is about steady readiness. A calm kind of confidence that comes from knowing you have taken the time to learn something that matters. The kind of readiness that doesn't need to shout. It simply says, I can help. I know what to do. I have practiced. I am not helpless. I am not guessing. I've got this.

That kind of skill might not show up on a résumé. It won't win you an award or draw applause. But it's useful in the most important way. It helps people. It protects life. It turns panic into action. It gives you the ability to make a real difference, right when it matters most.

You might never need it, or you might need it tomorrow.

And if you do, you'll be ready.

That is common sense.

Don't Post in Anger

At this point, posting online is second nature. It is built into our habits. It is how we share what we think, show what we do, and react to what we see. We post to celebrate, to complain, to connect, to be heard. It is a reflex now. Something we do without thinking too hard. One quick sentence, one click, and the whole world can see how we feel.

But just because it's easy does not mean it's always wise. Some things need more than a second. Some thoughts need time to settle. And some emotions, especially the heated ones, do not belong on display the moment they hit. A platform is not always the place to rush things. A post is not always the best version of what you have to say.

The internet is quick. One flick of a thumb and your words can fly across the world. In the heat of the moment, that feels powerful. It feels like a release. Like throwing a punch without leaving your chair. Like yelling into a megaphone that never runs out of battery.

But here's the thing. You should not post in anger.

Not because your anger is wrong. Anger can be honest. It can be sharp. It can be justified. But it is also a wildfire. It spreads fast. It burns everything in sight. And once you've hit send, you can't call the flames back. What felt like a spark can turn into damage. Real damage.

Posting in anger is like writing a message in permanent ink with a shaking hand. The emotions blur the edges. The judgment goes soft. And when you read it back, it often doesn't sound like you. It sounds like your worst moment, frozen and on display for the world.

You may think you are setting the record straight. Speaking truth to power. Putting someone in their place. And maybe that's part of it. But more often, you are just venting. Just trying to get something off your chest. Just hoping the pressure inside will drop if you let the words out fast enough.

And sometimes it does. For a minute.

But once it's out there, it's out there.

Screenshots live longer than apologies. Reactions come faster than understanding. What you meant in frustration can easily be taken as cruelty. Sarcasm reads as bitterness. Honesty sounds like aggression.

Online, people don't see your tone. They don't know your day. They don't feel the buildup behind your words. All they see is what you wrote.

And what you wrote becomes who you are, whether that's fair or not.

It is like throwing a message into the wind. Once it leaves your hands, you cannot control where it goes or how it is carried. The words leave your mouth, but after that, you lose control. You cannot control how they echo off the walls. You cannot control which part people hear first, or how loud it sounds from where they are standing.

Some might hear the whole thing. Others might hear only a piece. Some might twist it. Some might repeat it without context.

You cannot predict how people will take it. You cannot shape the meaning once it is out there.

And you definitely cannot decide what they will do with it afterward. They might share it. Judge it. Save it. Misunderstand it. It is no longer yours.

So pause.

Don't Post in Anger

Let the dust settle before you post. Let your heartbeat slow. Let your thoughts catch up with your feelings. Write it if you have to, but do not share it yet. Give it a night. Come back with clearer eyes. Often, when the emotion fades, the urgency disappears too.

You realize the post was more about being heard than being helpful. More about getting something off your chest than actually adding something useful to the conversation. More about being loud than being clear.

It was a reaction, not a response. A release of pressure, not a thoughtful contribution. And once the emotion fades, you start to see it for what it was. A moment of frustration dressed up as a message. Something that felt urgent in the moment but now just feels noisy.

You might still want to speak. That's fine.

Some things do need to be said. Some situations call for a response. But you will speak better when you are calm. When your mind has settled and your emotions have softened, your words become clearer. You are able to say what you mean without letting the heat distort the message. You are able to make your point without pushing people away.

Words spoken in anger usually make more noise than sense. They rattle, they sting, they echo in ways you did not intend. And once that noise is out in the world, you cannot mute it. You cannot gather it back up or soften the impact. It travels farther than you expect and lingers longer than you want. That's why it matters to wait. To breathe. To make sure your words carry weight, not just volume.

This is not about silencing yourself.

This is about being wise with timing. The internet doesn't forget. And it rarely forgives without lasting effects. Your words are not whispers. They are carved into a wall. Anyone can read them. And they often will not read them the way you meant them.

Think of your post like a letter that will be passed from hand to hand. Friends. Strangers. Future employers. People who do not know your heart. People who do not know the full story. You want that letter to reflect your values, not your outburst.

Anger wants speed. It wants to move before you think. It wants to strike fast, speak fast, react fast. It pushes you to punch first and deal with the consequences later. It convinces you that waiting is weakness and silence is surrender. But speed is not strength. Strength is holding yourself steady when your emotions are pulling at you.

Strength is knowing you could react, but choosing not to. Restraint is strength. Waiting is strength. Choosing stillness over reaction is strength. Letting the moment pass without jumping into it is not failure. It is maturity. It is wisdom. It is control.

The strongest voices are not always the loudest.

They don't rush to speak. They don't fill the silence just to be heard. They are the ones who wait until the right moment. The ones who understand that timing matters just as much as content. They choose their words with care. They think before they speak. They speak when it counts, not just when it feels good. They use words like a scalpel, not like a hammer. Their goal is not to break things, but to reveal something. Not to cause pain, but to cut through the noise and reach the point.

Not everything needs your opinion.

You don't have to weigh in on every issue. You don't have to share every thought the moment it comes to you. Not every insult deserves a reply. Not every rude comment needs a comeback. Not every error needs correction. Just because you notice something doesn't mean you are the one who needs to fix it.

Sometimes silence is not weakness. It is not backing down. It is not giving up. Sometimes it's control. It is choosing not to waste your energy. It is knowing when to speak and when to hold back. It is the quiet strength of someone who doesn't need to prove a point to know they are right.

There will be times when you need to speak up. Absolutely. But let it be on purpose, not on impulse. Let it come from clarity, not from chaos. Because once you post, it's permanent.

If you let anger lead, it will take you somewhere you don't want to go.

Do not post in anger.

Post when you are ready to be understood.

That is common sense.

Check the Source Before Sharing

We live in a world where news, rumors, and opinions can circle the planet in minutes. A headline flashes across your screen. A post pops up in your feed. A screenshot shows up in a group chat. Before you have even finished reading it, your finger is already hovering over the share button.

But not everything you see is true. Not everything is accurate.

And not everything is coming from someone who knows what they are talking about. Some of it is incomplete, leaving out details that matter. Some of it is twisted, reshaped to fit a certain angle or to stir up a reaction. Some of it is flat-out made up, with no truth in it at all. It is dressed up to look convincing, but beneath the surface there is nothing solid. It is shared again and again until it starts to feel real, even though it never was.

Once you share something, your name is attached to it.

It becomes part of your voice. You are vouching for it, whether you meant to or not. You are telling everyone who trusts you, "I believe this enough to pass it on." You are lending it your credibility. You are saying, "This is worth your time, your attention, and maybe even your agreement." And that means you should be sure. Because if it turns out to be wrong, you are not just passing along bad information. You are chipping away at the trust people have in you.

Checking the source is not about being cynical. It is not about doubting everything you see or distrusting everyone you know. It is about being responsible with what you choose to pass along. It is about protecting your own credibility so that when you do share something, people know they can take it seriously.

It is about making sure you are not helping bad information travel even further. Once something false is out in the world, it rarely disappears. False claims and half-truths spread quickly, often faster than the truth, and they can keep moving long after the facts have been clarified. They do not need your help to do damage.

So before you share, ask yourself some simple questions.

Who said this? Where did it come from? Is it the original source, or just someone repeating something they heard? Is there proof? Can you find the same claim backed up by a reliable outlet? If it's a screenshot, is there a link to the full post? If it's a photo, can you confirm it has not been taken out of context or edited? If it's a "fact," can you confirm it from somewhere that doesn't simply tell you what you already want to believe?

If you cannot answer those questions, you are not ready to share it.

Sharing without checking is like handing someone food without knowing whether it's safe to eat. You have no idea what's in it. You have not looked at it closely. You have not made sure it's good for them. Maybe it's fine. Or maybe it makes them sick. You would not want to be the reason someone swallowed something harmful, especially if it could have been avoided.

The same goes for information. If it is false, it does harm. It damages how people see the world. It can poison trust just as easily as bad food can poison the body, and once that trust is gone, it's not easy to get back.

The good news is that checking doesn't take too long.

Sometimes all it takes is searching for the headline in a browser. Or looking for the original source. Or checking if a reputable outlet is reporting the same story. You might find that the claim is missing key context. You might find that the photo is from ten years ago. You might find that the "quote" was never actually said by the person it's credited to.

Yes, checking slows you down. It breaks the rush of reacting and posting. It makes you pause instead of passing something along instantly. But that pause is the point. It is what stops bad information from spreading. It gives you time to be sure before you add your voice. If you care enough to share, care enough to check. The value of what you say is not in speed. It is in whether it holds up once someone looks closer.

Be careful with emotion-driven posts.

Anger, excitement, and fear all push you to act fast. They grab your attention and insist this is the moment to speak, to respond, to join in. They make it feel urgent, like if you do not act now you will miss your chance.

But urgency is a trick. It skips the step that matters most: thinking. Taking a breath. Asking if what you are about to share is true, complete, and worth passing on. Strong emotions are not the problem. The problem is when emotions take over and accuracy is left behind.

The faster you react, the more likely you are to pass along something false. A quick click can turn into a lasting mistake. A short pause can be the difference between spreading truth and spreading trouble.

It is not about being perfect. Everyone can get fooled. Even the most careful person can share something they later find out is wrong. Mistakes happen, and they will happen again.

The difference is that careless people spread false information because they never paused to check. They see, they react, they send it on without a second thought. There is no pause, no question, no moment of doubt.

Responsible people slow down. They take that extra step. They verify before they share. They make sure they are not adding to the noise or making the problem worse. They protect their own credibility by protecting the truth.

Checking the source before you share does not make you dull. It does not take away your voice or your relevance. It shows that you value truth over speed and accuracy over impulse.

It makes you someone people can rely on.

When you speak, others know you have taken the time to be sure. They know your words are backed by care, not just reaction. They know you are not in the habit of spreading things without knowing if they are true. And over time, that builds a trust that is worth far more than being the first to hit "share."

The truth already has a hard time keeping up with the speed of rumors.

False stories move faster, reach farther, and stick longer than facts. Once they take hold, they are hard to pull out. The truth has to work twice as hard just to catch up.

Do not help the lies spread.

Give the truth a real chance to be heard.

Share only what deserves to be repeated.

That is common sense.

Ask Questions When You Don't Understand

It takes courage to stop a conversation and say, "I am not sure I understand. Can you explain that?"

It feels easier to nod along. To stay quiet. To hope you will figure it out later. We have all been there, in a meeting, in a class, in a conversation with friends, hearing something we do not fully understand. We hesitate. We tell ourselves it's not the moment to ask.

In a meeting, someone races through a new process. Charts flash. Numbers roll. Instructions fly faster than you can write. You follow most of it, but one step does not make sense. You know it matters, but you are not sure how it works. You could ask and get clarity in seconds. Or you could stay silent and hope it makes sense later. It rarely does.

In class, the teacher moves fast. They write the new concept on the board, say it once, and move on. You catch some of it, but not all. One missing piece blocks the rest. You could raise your hand and ask. Or you could stay quiet and let the confusion build, even though it will only get harder to follow from here.

In conversation, a friend uses a term you have never heard before. It is small, just a passing reference, but it leaves you wondering what it means. You could simply say, "What does that mean?" and have them explain it in a few words. Or you could smile and pretend you know, letting the moment pass while you quietly stay in the dark. Most likely, you will smile and pretend you know.

Those moments may feel small, but they decide whether you leave the conversation informed or still in the dark.

The fear is almost always the same. You don't want to interrupt. You don't want to look slow. You don't want to be the one who admits not understanding what everyone else seemed to get. But looking uncertain for a few seconds is nothing compared to the frustration of staying confused. The awkwardness fades quickly. The understanding lasts.

The truth is, asking questions is a sign you care.

It shows you are paying attention, not just hearing words but actually trying to understand them. It shows you are present in the moment and not letting things pass you by without thought. It shows you are engaged enough to want the full picture, not just a rough outline.

Some people look confident because they never ask questions.

But silence does not always mean certainty. It might mean guessing. It might mean fear of looking slow. The ones who ask questions are often the ones paying closest attention. They take the time to clear confusion before it turns into a mistake. That small moment often saves them from bigger problems later.

Picture someone starting a new job. On day one, the manager explains a dozen procedures in under an hour. How to log in. How to file reports. How to handle client calls. How to respond in an emergency. Most of it lands. But one step is unclear. A small detail, easy to miss. But it connects to everything that follows.

The new hire could speak up. One simple question, answered in less than a minute. That moment of clarity would shape every task that comes after. The work would go smoothly. Confidence would grow.

But if the question stays quiet, the gap stays open. Two weeks later, the mistake has repeated itself. Now there is a backlog to fix. There is an awkward talk with the manager. There is stress that did not need to happen.

What could have been solved in seconds has now cost hours.

Or picture a student in math class. The teacher explains a formula, moving quickly from one step to the next. Most of it makes sense, but one part doesn't click. The student hesitates and decides to figure it out later.

But if the question is asked in that moment, the answer brings clarity. The next lesson makes sense. The work stays manageable.

If the question stays unasked, the confusion spreads. Each new step builds on that missing piece. By the end of the month, it is not just one formula that feels hard. It is the whole subject. Catching up feels out of reach.

Even in everyday life, the choice is the same. A friend says, "Meet me at the usual place." You pause. Do they mean the coffee shop near work? The park you used to walk through last fall? You could ask and clear it up in one sentence. Or you could guess, hoping you are right, and end up sitting in the wrong spot while they wait somewhere else. Now you are both frustrated, all because of a question that felt too small to ask.

Questions take seconds. Mistakes caused by not asking can take much longer to fix.

When you do ask, be clear. Give the person helping you a starting point.

If all you say is, "I do not get it," the other person has to guess what part you are confused about. That guess can lead to a long, unfocused explanation that still does not touch the thing you really needed to know.

Instead, aim for something specific, like, "Can you explain the part about how the total is calculated?" or "Can you go over the step where we enter the data?" This shows that you have been listening, that you have followed most of what was said, and that you just need help with one particular piece. It makes it far easier for the other person to give you exactly what you need without going in circles.

Ask Questions When You Don't Understand

And when the answer comes, listen closely.

Be specific when you ask. Stay focused when you listen. That is how a quick exchange becomes something that actually helps. It is how you leave with real answers, not just the same confusion wrapped in new words.

Do not think ahead to your next question. Do not drift while they are still speaking. Stay with them from start to finish. Clarity often comes at the end, and if you stop listening too soon, you miss the part that matters most.

Asking questions changes how people see you.

It shows you value clarity over pretending. It shows you are willing to speak up rather than let small misunderstandings grow into bigger problems. Over time, people trust someone who asks good questions more than someone who never does.

It also changes how you see yourself.

You stop thinking of asking as weakness and start seeing it as a tool. You realize the small discomfort of speaking up is a fair trade for the confidence that comes from understanding what is going on.

You do not have to question everything.

You just have to speak up when clarity matters.

Do not let confusion sit there and grow roots. The longer you wait, the harder it is to ask. The harder it is to fix. If you can get an answer now, get it. Save yourself the guesswork. Save yourself the mess later.

The people who grow the most are not the ones who never get lost. They are the ones who stop and ask for directions when they do.

If you want to be sure, ask. If you want to learn, ask. If you want to avoid mistakes, ask.

Tools for Life

The smartest people are not the ones with all the answers.

The smartest people are the ones who are willing to say, "I do not understand. Can you explain?"

Be that person.

That is common sense.

Read the Instructions

Some mistakes are born from ignorance. Others from pride. And then there are the ones that happen simply because you did not bother to read the instructions.

You know the feeling.

You dive in, confident you will figure it out as you go.

A piece of furniture that looks simple enough to assemble. A recipe that seems straightforward. A new gadget that must work like all the others. It all feels familiar, so why waste time reading a bunch of dry steps when you could just start? Skipping ahead feels faster. It feels like you are saving time.

Then it happens.

A screw goes in the wrong hole. The cake comes out flat. The gadget beeps angrily and refuses to work. You pause, trying to figure out where you went wrong. You flip through the instructions, hoping for a quick fix.

But by now the mistake has cost you more time than it would have taken to get it right from the start. What felt like a shortcut turned into a detour, and the extra effort you tried to avoid is now twice as hard to ignore.

Instructions exist for a reason. They are not there to slow you down or make the task more complicated than it needs to be. They are there because someone who has already been through the process knows where the mistakes usually happen. That person is trying to help you avoid them.

Every line is there to save you time, not waste it.

Someone else already figured out the best order, the right

measurements, the exact sequence that works. Following the instructions is the closest thing to having an expert guide you step by step, pointing out the little details you might otherwise miss. It is their way of saying, "Do it like this, and you will get it right the first time."

Still, there is a part of us that resists. Reading the instructions feels slow. It feels like the boring part before the real work begins. We tell ourselves, "I'll just figure it out." We picture ourselves as the kind of person who can figure anything out on instinct, someone who can just dive in and make it work without being told how.

And sometimes, yes, it goes that way. Sometimes you guess right, skip the reading, and everything falls into place.

But more often, the confidence is false. You are not saving time. You are just setting yourself up for extra work. You push ahead thinking you are being efficient, only to find yourself stopping, backtracking, and trying to undo a mistake that could have been avoided entirely.

It is not only about saving time.

It is about avoiding frustration.

There is a special kind of frustration that comes from knowing you could have avoided the mistake. All it would have taken was a few minutes of preparation. The problem was not inevitable. It did not have to happen at all.

You are not just irritated at the situation. You are irritated at yourself. You replay the moment when you skipped over the instructions or brushed off the chance to learn what you needed to know. You see how simple it would have been to get it right from the start. And that self-inflicted frustration lingers longer than the problem itself.

Cooking is a perfect example. The difference between a smooth dinner and a kitchen mess often comes down to one simple habit.

Did you read the recipe all the way through before starting? If not, you might realize halfway in that something needed to marinate for an hour. Or that the oven should have been preheated. Now you are waiting, improvising, and feeling the stress rise. All because you skipped the first step.

The same is true in bigger, more serious situations. Filling out legal forms. Setting up new technology. Starting a new job. The stakes are higher, and so are the consequences of skipping the instructions. Missing one detail can mean delays, extra work, or even losing an opportunity entirely.

Some people see instructions as limiting.

They feel like rules that box you in, telling you there is only one way to do something. They want to be creative and do things their own way. To put their own spin on it from the very start.

And there is a place for that.

Creativity works best when you understand the rules you are breaking. You can bend them, stretch them, or leave them behind, but only once you know what they are and why they exist. Reading the instructions gives you a solid foundation. It makes your choices intentional, not accidental. You are creating from understanding, not guessing.

Sometimes the "instructions" are not even written. They are spoken. A teacher tells you exactly what will be on the test. A client explains what they want in a project. A friend tells you what they need in a hard moment. Ignore these, and you are missing the map. Listening is just another way of reading the directions.

Here's the thing. Most instructions take less time to read than you think. Not an hour. Not even half an hour. Often it is five minutes. Maybe ten. That small investment can save you hours of fixing, redoing, or starting over.

Yes, some instructions are terrible. They can be confusing. They can be incomplete. Or they can be so badly translated that you have to read them twice just to guess what they mean. Sometimes they leave out steps entirely or assume you already know things you do not.

When that happens, you supplement. You look up a video. You ask someone who has done it before. You find an example you can follow. You gather whatever pieces you need to fill the gaps.

But even then, starting with what is given gives you a baseline. It shows you the intended path, even if it's not perfectly clear. It gives you a rough map so that when you bring in extra sources, you are filling in details rather than wandering without any direction at all.

And over time, this habit shapes you. You become someone who pauses before acting. Someone who plans, prepares, and avoids unnecessary trouble.

Sure, there is a little thrill in figuring things out without help. But most of the time, skipping the instructions just means you will be taking it all apart and starting over.

There is a simple rhythm to doing things well:

Pause.

Read.

Understand.

Then act.

You would not start a road trip without glancing at the map.

Even if you know the general direction, you still want to see the route. The turns. The distance ahead. You would not play a game without knowing the rules. Without them, you would not know how to score, how to win, or even how to take a proper turn.

So why take on real-life tasks without first learning the steps? A few minutes of preparation can save you from wrong turns, wasted effort, and confusion that never needed to happen. That small investment pays for itself as soon as you begin.

Reading the instructions is not about blind obedience.

It is about giving yourself a fair start. It is about respecting the process and avoiding problems you could see coming. It is one of the simplest habits you can build. And it pays off every single time.

So next time you are tempted to skip it, remember this.

Five minutes of reading now is almost always better than hours of fixing later.

That is common sense.

Being Busy ≠ Being Productive

We live in a culture that celebrates busy.

Packed schedules. Endless to-do lists. Days filled from morning to night. And still, it never feels like enough.

People wear busyness like a badge, as if the number of things they are doing automatically proves they are doing well.

But being busy is not the same as being productive. Busyness is often just noise that hides the lack of real progress.

You can fill every hour of your day and still move no closer to what actually matters. You can run in circles and end up exactly where you started. Activity is not the same as progress.

There is a certain comfort in busyness.

If you are always moving, always responding, always ticking something off a list, it feels like you are accomplishing a lot. It feels safe. It feels like proof you are working hard. But sometimes you are just avoiding the things that matter most. The hard work. The decisions you have been putting off. The deep thinking that requires time and focus.

It is like paddling furiously in a canoe that is tied to the dock. You are sweating. You are working. You are exhausted. Your arms ache from the constant strain, your back tightens with every stroke. The water ripples and churns beneath you, yet you are going nowhere. The rope stays taut, holding you in place, mocking every ounce of energy you pour into the effort.

But you are still in the same place.

Productivity is different. Productivity is about results. It is about identifying what matters most and then putting your energy into that. It is about asking, *If I only had two hours today, what would I focus on?* and then making sure those two hours are spent on something that actually moves you forward.

Busy is measuring effort and time. Productivity is measuring impact.

Imagine a desk covered in papers. You could spend an hour shuffling them around, making piles, and feeling busy the whole time. The motion feels productive. The desk looks different. But nothing important has actually moved forward.

Or you could take fifteen minutes to deal with the one paper that actually matters. The one that has been sitting there, silently blocking everything else. Clearing it frees up more than your desk. It removes the bottleneck that has been weighing on your mind and slowing down your day.

The same is true for your calendar. You can pack it with meetings, calls, and errands until there is no space left to think. No space to create. The days feel full, but the work that matters most keeps getting pushed to later. And later. And later.

Or you can choose to protect your time. Guard it like something scarce. Make room on purpose for the work that matters most. The projects. The decisions. The things that move the needle.

Real productivity is not about how much you do. It is about whether the important things actually get done.

A busy day might mean back-to-back meetings, a flood of emails, and a long list of small tasks. You are drained by the end of it, but you can't name a single thing that truly mattered.

A productive day might look quieter. Fewer hours. Fewer distractions. Fewer moving parts. But the thing that counted got done. You finished the proposal. You made the decision. You solved the problem that had been holding everything else back.

Busy is a full calendar. Productivity is a full life.

Sometimes we mistake motion for meaning. We feel important when the phone keeps buzzing and the inbox is full. We tell ourselves that the stress proves we are doing something valuable.

But stress is not success. And motion is not progress.

Think about a hamster on a wheel. It runs all day. Legs pumping. Never stopping. From its point of view, it is working hard. But it is going nowhere. That is what busyness can become: a wheel that spins without taking you forward.

A productive person may take fewer steps. But each one moves them in the right direction and closer to their goal.

One trap of busyness is that it feels easier than real productivity. Productivity asks you to stop and choose what actually matters. It forces you to face the work that moves things forward. That kind of work is harder. It takes more focus. It cannot be done half-distracted while checking your phone.

Busyness, on the other hand, feels safe. You can fill the day with little tasks and avoid the big one that scares you. You stay moving, but not advancing.

It is like cleaning your desk when you know you should be studying. You feel busy. You feel useful. But you are not doing the thing that counts.

Another danger is that busyness steals the time you need to think. Big ideas do not show up while you are answering emails every five minutes. Real solutions rarely appear when your mind is split across a dozen small tasks.

Productivity needs empty space. You need moments with nothing on the schedule. That is when your mind starts to see clearly. That is when the real work begins.

This is why some of the most effective people guard their time.

They say no to meetings that do not matter. They ignore emails that do not need a reply. It is not about being rude. It is about protecting their focus.

Ask yourself at the end of the day, *Did the things I worked on today actually matter?*

If the answer is no, then it doesn't matter how many hours you worked. Or how tired you feel. Effort alone is not the measure. What matters is whether the work was worth doing.

Think about steering a boat. You can stay busy scrubbing the deck, adjusting the sails, and polishing the railings. But if you are headed in the wrong direction, none of it matters.

Productivity is checking the compass. It is making sure the boat is pointed where you actually want to go.

Busyness keeps you moving, but without direction. You stay in motion, crossing things off, filling the hours, but not necessarily moving closer to anything that matters. It feels active, but it's aimless.

This is why it helps to stop and ask yourself: *What actually moves the needle? What will matter a month from now? What will still matter a year from now?*

These questions cut through the noise. They help you separate the urgent from the important. The distractions from the decisions that shape your future.

Answer them honestly, and you give yourself a compass.

You stop pouring energy into tasks that only feel important. You start focusing on the ones that actually move things forward.

You shift from chasing activity to building results.

And that is how real progress begins.

Sometimes being productive means doing less. It means crossing things off your to-do list not because you finished them, but because you realized they don't matter. It means replacing ten small tasks with one big task that truly matters.

It can even mean doing nothing for a while. Rest is productive when it restores your ability to focus. Clarity is productive when it saves you from spending weeks going in the wrong direction. Sometimes the most productive choice is to pause, step back, and make sure you are still on the right path

The difference is intention. Busy is reactive. You do whatever appears in front of you. Productive is intentional. You choose what matters and you give it your attention.

Think about a builder. A busy builder picks up every tool, hammers every nail, and saws every board without a plan. They stay in motion all day, but at the end, nothing fits together. A productive builder follows the blueprint. They measure twice, cut once, and focus on the pieces that hold the structure in place. That is how you get a solid house instead of a scattered pile of wood.

Busy is about filling time. Productivity is about making time count.

One of the hardest things is learning to say no to work that looks useful but is not important. People will always try to give you more to do. If you measure yourself by busyness, you will keep saying yes. If you measure yourself by productivity, you will start asking, *Will this actually matter?* and sometimes the answer will be no.

When you focus on what matters most, you will have less to show on paper. Fewer tasks. Fewer meetings. Less time spent rushing around. But what you do have will matter more. You will have results.

And results are what count.

Busy is easy to fake. Productivity is not.

One is about movement. The other is about direction. One is about hours worked. The other is about progress made.

The goal is not to fill your life with motion. The goal is to fill it with meaning.

That is common sense.

Your Phone Is a Tool, Not a Leash

Your phone is one of the most powerful tools you own.

In seconds, it can connect you to almost anyone. It can answer questions, settle debates, and pull up more information than any person in history ever had at their fingertips. It can guide you through a city you have never seen. It can help you find a coffee shop, translate a menu, or check how late the buses run.

It can store your memories. It can track your steps, your heart rate, your sleep. It can remind you of birthdays, appointments, and deadlines. It can plan your day, play your music, and wake you up in the morning.

It is a camera that can freeze a moment and hold it forever. It is a calendar that keeps your time in order and reminds you before things slip away. It is a map that can take you anywhere, whether across the city or across the world.

It is a notebook that captures ideas the moment they appear. It is a library in your pocket, ready to teach you something new at any hour. It is a megaphone that carries your voice to people on the other side of the planet.

It helps you stay on track so plans stay clear and details do not fall through the cracks. It keeps connections alive by making it easy to share life as it happens. It keeps things moving by tracking progress, offering reminders, and showing the way forward when everything feels uncertain.

It can do almost anything. And that's exactly why it can so easily take over everything.

But a tool is meant to be used with purpose. It is not meant to run your life.

Too often, the phone stops being something picked up with intention and becomes something opened without thought. Not because there is a real need, but because the screen lit up. Or because boredom crept in. Or simply because it's there.

It slips into the quiet moments. Standing in line. Sitting at a red light. Waiting for water to boil.

It slips into the middle of other activities. Between sentences in a conversation. During a commercial. While walking from one room to another.

The motion becomes automatic. Unlock. Scroll. Tap.

It is reflex, not intention.

And when that happens, it stops acting like a tool and starts behaving like a leash.

The choice of when to look is no longer made by the person holding it. The phone decides. Every alert interrupts whatever is in front of the eyes. Every vibration slices through the moment. Every bright little dot on an app hints at something waiting to be seen right now. Before long, the habit forms. The hand reaches for the screen without thought. The screen wakes from habit, not intention.

It becomes less about choosing to check and more about reacting automatically. The phone doesn't wait for a quiet moment. It interrupts the one already happening.

It is like carrying a bell that anyone in the world can ring at any time. No matter where the day has gone, someone else can pull the focus away from it. Eating dinner, and the bell rings. Midway through a conversation, and the bell rings. Deep in a task that needs concentration, and the bell rings. Each time, the flow is broken. The mind shifts to somewhere else entirely.

And it is not just messages.

Social media can turn that bell into a siren. Every like, every comment, every new post is designed to call attention, to make it feel urgent. The mind begins to expect these small jolts, and before long, the scroll becomes second nature. Hours pass without much to show for them.

The problem is not always the content itself. Articles, photos, videos, and updates can all be interesting. Some are even useful. They can be fun to watch, pleasant to scroll through, or worth sharing with someone else. It makes sense why they draw your attention. They are made to be engaging. They offer something new every time you look. That is part of what makes them appealing.

The problem is when the content sets the rhythm of the day. When the stream of updates and notifications becomes the clock, everyone follows. When the pace is decided not by plans, priorities, or real needs, but by whatever happens to appear on the screen next.

It is the difference between choosing what to focus on and being pulled along by whatever comes first. The phone starts leading. The person starts following. And the hours shape themselves around someone else's schedule, not their own.

Every spare moment becomes an invitation. Check. Refresh. Repeat.

Not because there is something urgent. But because the habit fills the space before anything else can.

Think about how other tools work. A hammer doesn't call out every few minutes, reminding anyone nearby that it exists. A measuring tape doesn't roll itself out while a conversation is going on. A map doesn't demand to be opened in the middle of dinner.

A tool stays where it is until it is needed. It waits quietly. It does nothing until the moment comes when it has a job to do.

A phone can do the same. It can wait on a desk, in a pocket, or in another room, ready to be used when there is a reason. But that only happens if it's treated that way. If it's picked up with intention instead of out of habit, and put down without the constant pull to check "just in case."

This is about control.

When the phone is in control, the day is shaped around its interruptions. Time disappears into quick checks that turn into long scrolls. Focus frays. Conversations lose their depth. Small moments slip away without being noticed.

When the person is in control, the phone stays powerful, but it's not in charge. It serves the day instead of shaping it. Social media can be opened with intention and enjoyed for twenty minutes. Then it ends because you chose to stop. Not because the app ran out of things to show.

The phone can be left on a table for an hour without the constant pull to check it. Notifications can wait until the right time, instead of cutting into every task and conversation. The phone is still part of life, but it no longer sits in the driver's seat.

A phone that acts like a leash doesn't just take time. It takes attention. It pulls focus away from the people and places that deserve it most. And the cost is subtle but real.

Picture a conversation with a friend. The phone lights up on the table, and eyes shift for just a second. That second is enough to miss the pause before their next words. The look in their eyes. The detail in their tone. Being there, but not fully there.

It adds up. Tiny shifts in attention leave your mind scattered. A full day can pass, but without feeling lived.

And that's no accident. The pull of the phone is intentional, built to keep you hooked.

Tools for Life

Teams of designers and engineers work to make it irresistible. Platforms are built to reward constant checking, to create the feeling of missing something if the app is not opened.

That's why boundaries are not optional. They are necessary.

Boundaries can be simple. Silence nonessential notifications so the screen stays dark. Leave the phone in another room during meals or conversations so your attention stays with the people in front of you. Set specific times to scroll and keep them. Don't let the feed creep into every pause.

These are small changes, but they create space. Space to think. Space to be present. Space to live without the constant hum of a device always asking for attention.

A tool waits until it's picked up. A leash pulls whether the person is ready or not.

A phone can be either.

It can serve as the camera that captures a memory worth keeping. The library that answers a question at the perfect moment. The map that guides the way to somewhere new. The clock that keeps the day on track. The translator that makes it possible to communicate across languages.

Or it can run your life without permission.

Your attention is worth more than that.

Your time is worth more than that.

Your life is worth more than that.

That is common sense.

You Don't Need to Respond Right Away

In the last chapter, we looked at how the phone can start running the day instead of the person holding it. How every buzz and light can pull attention away from the moment that actually matters.

The habit usually begins with the need to reply instantly. Or maybe just the perceived need.

Somewhere along the way, the idea took hold that instant replies are a sign of respect. That the faster the answer, the more it proves someone cares. That replying within seconds means being a good friend, a good colleague, a good partner, a good person.

It became an unspoken rule, reinforced by every read receipt, the little "typing..." indicator, and "seen at" timestamp. The moment a message is opened, the clock starts ticking. If the reply doesn't come quickly, it can be taken as a sign of disinterest, neglect, or offense. Even when none of that is true.

But speed is not the same as care.

Very few things in daily life require an immediate response. Most messages are not urgent. Most questions can wait. Most notifications do not need to pull someone out of what they are doing right now.

Still, the moment the phone lights up, it feels urgent. That little ping hits like a knock on the door. The kind you feel you must answer right away. But this is not someone standing in the rain. It is just a line of text. And it will be exactly the same five minutes from now.

The urgency is artificial. The choice is still yours.

There is a difference between being available and being on call for everyone at all times.

When life is lived in constant reply mode, the mind is never fully here. Attention stays divided, leaning toward the next buzz, ping, or flash on the screen.

A conversation with the person in front of you turns patchy, broken into pieces between screen checks. A task that needed focus gets chopped apart. Every interruption makes it harder to return to where you left off.

Even rest feels lighter. Because part of your mind is still busy. Rehearsing a reply. Wondering how your words will land. Already halfway into the next response.

Pausing before answering is not disrespect. It is a choice to give full attention to one thing at a time.

When a message arrives, it's easy to feel that spark of urgency. But that feeling isn't a signal of importance. It's just a reflex.

Waiting, even for a short time, does a few important things. It creates space to think about what to say. It prevents sending a reply that will need correcting later. And it lets you stay present in your own moment, instead of being pulled into someone else's timeline.

It also sets a quiet boundary. It tells the world, and yourself, that your time is yours to manage. That you will respond, but you will choose when.

And the people who matter will understand.

This doesn't mean ignoring messages for days or leaving people hanging on purpose. It means understanding that every single thing that appears on the screen does not automatically take priority over the person, place, or work right in front of you.

Think about the difference in quality. A rushed reply might be fast, but it often misses the point. It might forget to answer a question, skip an important detail, or carry the wrong tone. A reply written after a short pause often has more thought, more clarity, and more care.

It is like answering a question in a meeting before you have finished hearing it. You might speak quickly, but you might also be wrong.

Sometimes waiting to respond is not even for thinking. It is simply for staying with what is already happening. To stay in the conversation that is happening face to face, without letting it be replaced by the one on a screen.

It is for finishing what you were doing. Completing the sentence you were writing. Listening until the other person is done speaking. Reaching the end of the task you were focused on.

The reply still gets sent. But it happens after the moment you are in has run its course. Not the moment the phone lights up and interrupts it.

And here is something worth remembering: most people do not actually expect you to respond immediately. Many of them are sending their message and moving on with their own day. The only person creating the pressure is often you.

Of course, there will be exceptions. Emergencies happen. Some things cannot wait. But they are rare enough to stand out when they do. That is why it's worth breaking the habit of treating everything as if it falls into that category.

Consider a few everyday moments.

A text arrives during dinner. You could reply right away and split your attention between the table and the screen. Or you could let it wait until the meal is done, giving your full attention to the people you are with.

An email pings in while you are writing. You could switch over instantly, lose your train of thought, and spend twice as long getting back into it. Or you could finish the paragraph, send the reply later, and keep the flow of your work intact.

A friend sends a photo in the middle of a movie. You could unlock the phone, check it, type something back, and miss part of the scene. Or you could enjoy the photo after the credits roll.

In each case, the world does not fall apart because you waited.

What starts to fall apart, slowly and quietly, is your ability to be fully present. When every small beep gets treated like a fire alarm, your focus is constantly pulled away. You are no longer fully in the moment you are in. You are always halfway somewhere else.

The truth is, the gap between when a message is sent and when it is read is almost never the problem. Most messages are fine sitting for a while before they are answered.

The real problem is the belief that the gap should be zero.

It is the idea that nothing is more important than the thing that just appeared on the screen. It is the idea that whatever is happening right now should step aside for it, no matter how small or unimportant it might be.

Choosing not to respond right away is not laziness. It is prioritizing. It is deciding that the thing in front of you deserves your full attention before you move on to something else. It is protecting the current moment from being replaced too soon by a different one.

It is a way of showing that the moment in front of you matters. The conversation you are having. The work you are doing. The rest you are giving yourself. It means letting each moment have its place instead of allowing every new notification to shove it aside.

And here is something else. When your response is always instant, you create a pattern. People start to expect it. They begin to assume you are always available. Then the rare moment you do not reply right away feels like something is wrong, even though it is simply normal.

Breaking that pattern is part of taking control back. It is a reminder that you decide how and when to respond, not the device in your hand. Respond at a pace that works for you, one that fits into your life instead of constantly interrupting it.

Do it consistently, and people adjust. Soon that pace becomes the expectation. The pressure to be instant fades, replaced by a rhythm that feels sustainable and deliberate.

Instant is not the same as important.

Fast is not the same as good.

Most people will not remember how quickly you replied.

They will remember what you said and whether it mattered.

That is common sense.

Reputation Is Like Glass: Easy to Break, Hard to Fix

You might not think about it every day, but your reputation is always working in the background. It shapes how people experience you. It follows you into every room, even when you say nothing.

You do not get to control what people think, but your actions, your words, your choices, and your habits all tell a story. And over time, that story becomes your reputation.

Reputations are not built in grand moments.

Reputations are built in the quiet, repetitive decisions that seem small at the time. Like showing up when you say you will. Following through on commitments, even when no one is watching. Choosing honesty, not because it's convenient, but because it's right. Being kind to people who cannot offer you anything. Staying calm in moments when it would be easier to snap.

None of that makes headlines. But it makes a name.

You do not need to be perfect. No one is.

What matters more than any single moment is the pattern you create over time. People do not remember every word you say or every task you complete. But they remember how you made them feel. They remember whether you were consistent, whether they could trust you, and whether your values held up when things got hard.

Trust is not built in grand gestures, but in the small, steady pattern of your actions. Quietly. Patiently.

But here is the hard part. A single careless moment can undo a lot of that work. A lie. A betrayal. A mean comment said in anger. A broken promise you never bothered to explain. People do not forget moments like those.

While some damage can be repaired, the crack never quite disappears. It is possible to recover, but it often takes more time than you expect. Sometimes much more than you expect.

So yes, you can fix bad reputation. But the repair takes time. And even then, there may still be a scar.

That is why reputation is worth protecting. Not with fear or people-pleasing. But with integrity. With awareness of the weight your name carries, even when you are not in the room.

We live in a time when reputations can be made or broken faster than ever. One thoughtless decision, captured and shared, can reach thousands of people in minutes. A single screenshot, taken out of context or not, can follow you for years. One careless post. One cruel joke. One burst of anger. And suddenly, something you said or did in ten seconds becomes a permanent part of how people see you.

This isn't just about social media or public figures. It happens in everyday life too. An angry email sent too quickly. A text message captured in a screenshot and shared. A rumor whispered in a group chat. Once it's out there, it spreads. And often, you don't get the chance to explain or undo it.

Reputation is not just about image. Reputation is about trust.

Once people start to question your character, they pull back. They become cautious. The same people who once gave you the benefit of the doubt now hesitate. Sometimes it's not because they want to judge you, but because they no longer feel safe letting their guard down.

Trust is built in layers and moments, and when it's taken for granted, it disappears faster than most people realize.

But it is not just about big scandals or public mistakes.

Most damage to reputation happens in smaller, quieter ways. Being unreliable. Being known for gossip. Showing up late all the time. Taking credit for other people's work. Acting one way when people are watching, and another when they are not. These things might seem small on their own, but over time, they paint a picture. And eventually, people stop giving you the benefit of the doubt.

Think about someone in your life whose word carries weight. When they say they will do something, you do not wonder. You know they will follow through.

When they give their opinion, you listen. Not just out of politeness, but because you trust that they have thought it through. Their voice carries credibility, not because they are the loudest in the room or the most confident, but because they have proven themselves in quiet, consistent ways.

They meet deadlines. They follow through on commitments. They speak with honesty, not exaggeration. They give credit where it's due. And when they make a mistake, they own it.

That kind of reputation doesn't come from a single moment. It is built slowly, often invisibly, in situations where no one would have blamed them for cutting corners. But they didn't. They chose integrity, even when no one was watching.

Now think about someone else. Someone whose reputation makes you second-guess. Maybe they have let you down one too many times. Maybe they are friendly in person but speak differently when you are not around.

Maybe they shift the story when accountability shows up, or never quite accept their part when things go wrong. You might still smile when you see them. You might still keep the peace, especially in group settings or work environments.

But inside, something is different. Your guard is up. Your trust is thinner. You no longer take their words at face value. You double-check. You pause. You hesitate. And even if they do not realize it, the relationship has changed.

That is the quiet truth about reputation. When trust starts to fade, people rarely announce it.

Most of the time, they do not tell you they are pulling back. They just begin to act differently. Fewer invitations. Less involvement. Less openness. They keep things light, distant, surface-level. You may not notice at first. It might feel subtle. But it's there. The space grows gradually. And once it does, it's hard to shrink it again.

Reputation isn't about being perfect.

No one gets everything right. We all make mistakes. We all have days when we are tired, distracted, or not at our best. That is part of being human. What truly matters is not the occasional misstep, but the overall pattern.

The question is not whether you have ever slipped up, but how you carry yourself the rest of the time. Do your words align with your actions? Do you show up the way you say you will? When you fall short, do you take ownership or look for someone else to blame? Do people feel respected in your presence, even when there is nothing in it for you? Do they feel safe telling you the truth, even when it's uncomfortable?

Those are the things that shape your reputation over time. Not the one-off moments, but the steady pattern of how you choose to show up.

A strong reputation is like insurance.

It does not mean you will never face hard moments. But it does mean people are more likely to give you grace when you need it. If you have built trust, others are more willing to hear your side. They are more willing to believe that a bad moment was just that, a moment, not a reflection of your whole character.

You do not need everyone to like you.

Being liked by everyone is not the goal. Trying to be liked by everyone will only wear you out and pull you in too many directions.

What you want is to be known for something solid. To be known as someone who is honest. Someone who says what they mean and means what they say.

Someone who stays steady when things are tense. Who is fair, not just when it's easy, but when it's inconvenient.

You want your name to carry a sense of trust. Not because you are perfect, but because you are dependable.

You want people to know that if you give your word, you will follow through. That if you say something to their face, you will not say something different behind their back. That your behavior stays consistent, no matter who is watching. These traits may not win you applause. They may not get instant recognition. But over time, they earn something more valuable than attention. They earn respect.

That kind of reputation is not flashy. But it is rare. And it is worth protecting.

Protect your reputation. Guard it not by trying to control what others think, but by choosing to live with character, especially when no one is watching.

Speak carefully. Keep your word. Be mindful of how you treat people who have nothing to offer you.

Reputation is a reflection of who you are.

Reputation is like glass. It can be beautiful, clear, and strong. But once it shatters, even if you glue it back together, the cracks remain. So handle it with care.

Not to impress.

But to live with integrity.

That is not just good advice.

That is common sense.

PART FIVE

Keep Growing

Keep Growing

Growth is not a finish line. It is a practice. You learn, you try, and you collect small wins. Mistakes will happen, but they can teach you if you let them. Growth is choosing progress over perfection and showing up today to take the next step. Over time, those small steps add up to something meaningful. This chapter is about staying curious and moving forward one step at a time.

Stay Curious

Curiosity is the spark that keeps life interesting. It is what makes you lean in instead of tune out. It is what turns an ordinary day into something that might surprise you.

When you are curious, the world stays alive in front of you. You notice details other people miss. You ask questions that lead to better answers. You find connections between things that seem unrelated. You keep learning, even when no one is grading you.

Curiosity is not just for children, scientists, or artists. It is for anyone who wants to keep growing instead of quietly shrinking into routine.

The opposite of curiosity is not ignorance. It is assumption. It is the quiet voice that says, "I already know enough. I have seen it before. I have nothing new to learn here." That voice closes doors before you even know what is on the other side.

The antidote to that voice is curiosity. Stay curious.

Ask *why?* even when it seems obvious. Ask *how?* when someone shows you a skill. Ask *what if* when you are faced with a problem. Don't be afraid to look like you are still learning. Because you are. We all are.

When you are curious, you don't just pass through the world. You engage with it. You stop treating each day like a rerun of the one before. You start noticing when things shift, even in small ways. The same street you have walked a hundred times looks new. The shop window you always passed finally catches your eye.

Curiosity changes how you approach people too. You stop rushing to label and start wondering instead. You begin to ask what shaped their choices, what pressures they felt, what fears they might carry. You look past the opinion and try to see the person behind it.

Keep Growing

Instead of arguing to prove a point, you ask what made them see the world that way. You listen without planning your next response. You let them speak without jumping ahead in your mind. You stop assuming you already know who they are and give them the space to tell their own story. That small shift can change everything.

A curious person leaves space for surprise.

When you meet someone with a skill you do not have, ask them how they learned it. Not just "Where did you go to school?" but "What was the moment you first felt like you could really do this?" When you travel, notice the small habits that make life work in that place. How people greet each other, how they cook their food, how they end the day. When you read, go beyond the headlines. When you watch a film, ask what the director was trying to make you feel.

Curiosity is not just about gathering facts.

It is about noticing connections. It is about seeing that a skill you learned in one part of your life could help in a completely different area. It is about recognizing that a conversation with someone in a different field could spark an idea for your own work.

Curiosity also protects you from getting stuck. It keeps you from repeating the same patterns without noticing whether they still serve you.

The moment you stop being curious, you start living on autopilot. You do things the way you have always done them. Not because they are the best way. But because you stopped asking if there is a better one.

Think about workplaces. Some of the best ideas do not come from the loudest voice in the room, but from someone who asks a quiet question like, "Why do we do it this way?" That one question can uncover habits that no longer serve a purpose. It can reveal a shortcut that saves hours of work or shine a light on a process that no one ever thought to challenge. Maybe it's a new hire who notices that three different people are entering the same data in three different systems. Everyone else was too used to the routine to question it. Curiosity cuts through autopilot. It helps people see what has been overlooked. It makes space for something better.

Curiosity takes almost no extra time.

You can choose to ask instead of assume. You can choose to notice instead of rush past. You can choose to learn instead of just confirm what you already believe.

Each time you do this, you give yourself more room to grow. You open a window in your mind instead of recycling the same stale thoughts. Even a small question can shift the way you see something. That pause to ask *why?* or *how?* can turn an ordinary moment into something you carry forward.

The more you do it, the more natural it feels. Curiosity starts to work in the background. You look twice at things you once ignored. You notice patterns in the way people act. You see how problems form. You see how solutions appear when you change your angle.

You start making connections between ideas that once felt separate. You find that an insight in one area can help you in another. And with those patterns and connections come solutions you would have missed if you had only relied on what you already knew.

Being curious doesn't mean doubting everything or chasing every random fact. It doesn't mean turning every conversation into a research project. You don't have to become an expert in every topic that comes your way.

Curiosity is more about keeping your mind open enough to let the world in. It is about staying interested in how things work, why people choose what they choose, and what life looks like through someone else's eyes.

Keep Growing

Curiosity shows up in small ways.

You can ask the person at the coffee shop how they make a certain drink. You can ask a colleague how they organize their day. You can ask your friend what they were thinking when they chose the place you are eating dinner. These small questions open small doors. And enough small doors can change the way you move through the world.

Curiosity also shows up in big ways.

You can learn the history of the place you live. You can take a class in a subject you have always found intimidating. You can start a conversation with someone you think you have nothing in common with and find that you share more than you expected.

Sometimes curiosity means letting go of the need to be right. When you approach everything as if you already know, you block the chance to learn something new. But when you stay open, you create space for more. You give people a chance to surprise you, to challenge your thinking, to offer a piece of the puzzle you did not even know was missing. That is how learning happens. Not from holding your ground, but from being willing to explore.

Curiosity makes life richer.

A walk becomes more than just exercise when you notice the flowers changing with the season. A job becomes more than a paycheck when you ask why things are done a certain way and look for better ways to do them. A conversation becomes more than small talk when you ask the right question and really listen to the answer.

Curiosity also builds connection.

People can tell when you are genuinely interested in them.

When you ask thoughtful questions, they feel noticed. They feel valued. They open up in ways they might not have planned to.

Curiosity signals care. And that makes relationships stronger.

One of the easiest ways to build curiosity into your life is to follow a thread. When you come across something you do not understand, do not brush it off. Look it up. Ask someone. Read a little more about it.

Curiosity works like a chain. One question leads to another. Before you know it, you are somewhere you never expected to be, seeing the world with wider eyes.

Even boredom can be a signal. If you feel like you are moving through your days on autopilot, that might be your mind asking for something new to chew on. Try a new skill, a new hobby, or even a new route home. Curiosity often hides in these small shifts.

Of course, not every curiosity will lead to something big.

Some will fizzle out. You will follow a question, find the answer, and that will be enough. That is fine. What matters is not that every thread leads somewhere important, but that you keep pulling on them. The real value is in staying curious.

Children do this naturally.

They ask hundreds of questions a day without worrying how they sound. They ask what things are, how they work, and why they matter. They wonder about things adults have long stopped noticing. A shadow on the wall. The shape of a cloud. The sound a light makes when it flickers.

They are not embarrassed by what they do not know. They are curious. Open. Unfiltered.

But somewhere along the way, many of us lose that habit. We stop asking. We get busy. We get self-conscious. We worry about looking uninformed. We start thinking it is safer to act like we already know, even when we do not.

But staying curious keeps you from becoming too certain. Too rigid. Too closed off.

The world changes. People change. You change. Curiosity helps you keep up. It keeps your mind flexible, your thinking fresh, and your conversations alive.

Stay open. Listen.

Let yourself be surprised.

The world does not run out of things worth noticing.

The only thing that runs out is our willingness to look.

Stay curious.

Keep asking.

Keep exploring.

Keep learning.

That is common sense.

Read Beyond Your Interests

One place curiosity shows up is in the books you choose to read, and it is easy to stay inside your reading comfort zone.

You find a subject you like and keep going back to it. The same authors. The same genre. The same kind of ideas. You know what to expect. There is nothing wrong with that.

Familiar books can feel like trusted friends. They feel safe. They give you comfort. They make you feel at home. You can sink into them without effort because you already understand the style and rhythm. You know they will deliver what you are looking for. They do not challenge you too much or take you somewhere you do not want to go. You already know you will enjoy them.

But if you never step outside that comfort zone, you miss out on a lot.

Reading beyond your interests opens doors you did not know were there.

You might pick up a book on a topic you have never cared about, only to find yourself hooked by the way it changes how you see the world. You might read a biography of someone you thought had nothing to do with your life, only to discover a lesson that fits perfectly into it.

You might start a book thinking it's not for you, and finish it with a whole new set of ideas in your head.

When you read only within your usual topics, your mind gets used to moving in the same patterns. You reinforce what you already know. You stay in familiar territory. That is comfortable, but it's not where the most growth happens.

Reading beyond your interests challenges those patterns. It

Keep Growing

interrupts the loop of reading the same kind of thing over and over. It asks your mind to stretch in new directions.

It introduces you to ways of thinking you have not tried before. You might come across ideas that feel unusual or even uncomfortable at first. You might see familiar issues through a completely different lens.

It puts you in touch with stories you would never have lived and facts you would never have found on your own. It gives you glimpses into worlds that operate by different rules than the ones you know.

It reminds you that the world is bigger than your preferences. There are experiences you have not lived, perspectives you have not considered, and possibilities you have not explored. And some of them might end up mattering to you more than you ever expected.

And the benefits do not stop when you close the book.

The ideas follow you. They slip into your conversations. They shape the way you solve problems. One day you are tackling an issue at work, and a line from a completely unrelated book comes back to you. Suddenly you see the problem in a new way. Reading widely helps you connect fields most people would never think to link.

That is the power of variety.

You don't have to love everything you read. In fact, you probably will not. Some books will feel like a chore. Some will never fully click with you. But even then, they can give you something. A single paragraph that sticks with you. A new idea that sends you down a path you would not have found otherwise. A new term you had never heard before. A tiny shift in how you look at something.

And sometimes, the books you thought you would hate turn out to be the ones you remember the most.

You might be a fan of business books but end up deeply moved by a memoir. You might prefer novels but find a non-fiction book that makes you rethink a belief you have held for years. You might stick to history but stumble into a science book that leaves you in awe.

Reading beyond your interests is not about replacing what you love.

It is about adding to it.

It is about letting unfamiliar subjects challenge you. It is about giving your mind something different to work with, something that doesn't fit neatly into what you already know. Something that makes you pause. Something that forces you to stretch.

When you read beyond your interests, you borrow perspectives from worlds you have never lived in. You see problems and solutions from angles you would not have imagined on your own. You step into the thoughts of people whose lives are nothing like yours, and for a moment, you get to see as they see.

You add new tools to your thinking. You collect ideas, examples, and patterns that you can use later without even realizing where they came from.

You make connections that your usual reading list will never give you. The mix of unrelated subjects starts to overlap in your mind. New combinations form. Fresh ways of thinking emerge.

And none of it would have happened if you had stayed inside the same narrow space.

Sometimes the most useful idea you will ever get will come from a place you would never have looked on your own.

The point is not to force yourself into topics you find dull forever. It is to give them a fair chance. To see what they might offer you.

You might not think you care about astronomy until you read about how stars are born. You might not think you like poetry until a certain poem makes you stop and read it twice. You might not

Keep Growing

think you need to know anything about gardening until a book on growing food makes you rethink where your meals come from.

The beauty of reading is that it costs little to explore.

One trip to the library can give you access to dozens of worlds you have never visited. A quick download to your phone or e-reader can bring you a book you never would have bought otherwise. Even a free article online can plant an idea that changes the way you think about something.

If you are not sure where to start, let chance help you. Pick a random book from a section you never visit. Ask a friend for a recommendation in a genre you never touch. Read the first chapter and see where it takes you.

Sometimes you will stop halfway. That's fine. Not every book has to be finished. The point is not to tick boxes. The point is to give yourself the chance to be surprised.

This habit can also make you a better communicator.

The more you read, the more people you can connect with. You have more topics to talk about, more examples to draw from, more ways to relate. A conversation with a scientist might remind you of something from a novel. A discussion with an artist might echo a story you read about history. The dots start to connect in unexpected ways.

The more varied your reading, the more bridges you can build.

Reading beyond your interests also trains your brain to be more flexible. It gets used to switching between different kinds of thinking. It makes it easier to adapt when you face something unfamiliar in your own life.

Your reading habits shape your mental habits.

If you want to think in new ways, expose yourself to new ideas. If you want to understand more of the world, explore more of it through words.

There is another benefit. When you explore topics you do not know much about, you get to practice being a beginner again. You let go of the comfort of knowing and step into the openness of learning. You remind yourself what it feels like to start fresh, to ask questions.

You remember what it feels like to not have all the answers. You remember how to pay closer attention, how to notice details, and how to connect pieces together. You remember how to learn.

And that humility carries over into other parts of your life. It makes you more open to new experiences and more understanding toward others who are also finding their way.

So keep reading the things you love.

But every so often, reach for something different. Something unfamiliar. Maybe even something that seems boring at first.

Give it a real chance. Let it surprise you.

If you walk away with even one new idea, it was worth it.

Because the more you stretch beyond your usual interests, the more your world expands. You notice patterns you never saw before. You start connecting dots across fields that look completely unrelated. What once felt distant or irrelevant suddenly feels useful, even exciting.

That is how you grow.

That is how you keep your mind alive.

That is how you stay open to the world.

That is common sense.

Learn by Doing

You can read about something for weeks. You can take notes, highlight the important parts, and listen to hours of advice from people who know more than you. All of that can help. But it's not the same as rolling up your sleeves and trying it yourself.

Some things only make sense once you start doing them.

You can study how to swim, but until you get in the water, you do not really know what it feels like. You can watch videos on how to change a flat tire, but until you have actually loosened the bolts and wrestled the wheel off, it's just theory.

The moment you start doing something for real, the learning changes. It becomes less about what you think might happen and more about what actually does happen. Theories turn into choices you have to make in real time.

You stop imagining how it might work and start feeling what it's like to make it work. You notice things you never would have caught in a book or a video. The way a tool feels in your hand. The small signs that something is going right or going wrong. The rhythm that only comes with practice.

It will not always be smooth.

In fact, the beginning is often messy. You make mistakes. You feel clumsy. You forget what you thought you had memorized. But that's part of the process. Every mistake shows you something you could not have learned by just thinking about it.

Learning by doing builds a kind of knowledge that sticks. It is rooted in your own experience, not just borrowed from someone else's. When you have done something with your own hands, solved a problem in real time, or adjusted your approach mid-task, it leaves a mark you can come back to later.

Learn by Doing

Think about learning to ride a bike. You probably wobbled, overcorrected, and maybe even fell a few times. But each try taught you something: how to balance, how to steer, how to keep moving without tipping over. Those lessons stayed with you because you learned them in motion.

The same applies to skills in work, relationships, hobbies, and everyday life. You can read about having a difficult conversation, but you learn far more from actually having one. You can research gardening for months, but you will learn more from planting seeds, watching them grow, and figuring out why some plants thrived while others did not.

The fear of starting often keeps people stuck in the "thinking" stage. They want to feel completely ready before they begin. They want the perfect plan, the perfect timing, the perfect conditions. But real learning starts when you take action, even if you are not completely prepared.

Preparation is good. But over-preparation can be a way of avoiding the risk of actually trying.

You might be afraid to start because you will not be very good at it in the beginning. That is true. You probably will not. Almost nobody is. But that's not a reason to wait. It is a reason to start sooner. Every day you put it off is another day before you get through the shaky first attempts. The faster you get through the awkward stage, the faster you get better.

Think about anything you have ever learned to do well. At some point you were bad at it. You stumbled through the steps, forgot what came next, and felt clumsy. But each time you tried, you built a little more skill and a little more confidence. The only way past that stage is to go through it.

Doing teaches you things you cannot get from theory alone.

When you actually try something, you feel the weight of it. You learn how your body moves, how your mind reacts under pressure,

Keep Growing

and how your emotions shift when something doesn't go as planned. You learn how it feels to adjust on the spot. You learn how to recover when something goes wrong.

Even failure is valuable when you are learning by doing. You might not get the result you wanted, but you get the experience you needed. The next time you try, you will start from a stronger place.

There is also a confidence that comes from having done something yourself. You stop wondering if you *could* do it and start knowing you *can*. That confidence stays with you, and it often spreads into other parts of your life.

Sometimes you try something and realize you do not actually like it. That is still a win. You thought it would be exciting or fulfilling. You imagined it was exactly what you were looking for.

But once you are in it, you feel bored. Or drained. Or just off. That is not failure. That is clarity. You have learned something you could not have known from the outside.

You have saved yourself months or even years chasing something that doesn't fit. Now you can put that time and energy toward something that does.

The only way to know for sure is to try.

Learning by doing is also how you uncover shortcuts and tricks that books never mention. The details that make a job easier. The habits that make a skill second nature. The small adjustments that improve results.

It is not about skipping the basics. It is about reinforcing them through action.

Think of a new driver. Reading the manual is useful, but the real learning happens when they are behind the wheel, merging into traffic, and remembering to check their mirrors while keeping an eye on the road. The skill becomes more than information. It becomes muscle memory.

Or take learning a language. You can spend months memorizing vocabulary and grammar rules. But the moment you speak to a native speaker, everything changes. You learn how fast people talk. How they use slang. How they gesture while speaking. You will get words wrong. You might make someone laugh without meaning to. And you will remember those moments far more clearly than anything you read in a textbook.

That is how real learning happens. In the doing, not just the studying.

If you want to learn by doing, start small.

Pick one thing you have been meaning to try and take the first physical step. Sign up for a beginner class. Cook one new recipe. Try fixing something instead of throwing it away. Write a single page instead of planning a whole book.

Do not wait until you feel ready. Read enough to get started, then get started.

You might surprise yourself. You might even enjoy the process more than the result.

And when you look back, you will see it clearly. The awkward, uncertain attempts were when you learned the most. You had to pay attention. You had to adjust. You had to figure things out without a script. It was uncomfortable, but it built the instincts you now rely on without thinking. You may not have known it at the time, but those messy starts were laying the foundation. That is where progress began.

The knowledge you gain through action sticks. It goes deeper than something you just read or heard because you lived it. You felt the effort. You made the mistakes. You earned the small wins. You saw what worked and what did not. That kind of learning lasts. You trust it more because it's yours. Not borrowed. Not second-hand.

Keep Growing

Built through experience, one step at a time.

Learning is not just knowing what to do. It is knowing how it feels to do it. The rhythm. The flow. The unexpected moments that no lesson can fully prepare you for. That is the difference between understanding something in your head and carrying it in your bones.

You learn most by doing.

Skill is built from the inside, not the sidelines.

So when you are learning something new, start small. But step in fully.

That is where real learning begins.

That is common sense.

Practice Until It's Natural

You learn most things by doing. But doing something once is not enough.

The first time you try, it feels awkward. Your hands are clumsy. Your words stumble. Your mind hesitates between each step. You know what you're aiming for, but it doesn't come out the way you pictured it. That is normal.

Skill is not built in a single attempt.

It grows piece by piece. It is built through repetition, through showing up and doing it again even when it still feels awkward. Each time, you get a little smoother. Each time, your mind and body understand it a little better.

You do it again and again until it stops feeling strange and starts feeling familiar. Until the movements, the words, or the steps fit together without so much effort.

And then you keep going until it feels natural. Until it's no longer something you have to force. Until it becomes part of you. Until it becomes something you can do without having to remind yourself what comes next.

When something becomes natural, you no longer have to think about every small move.

You can focus on the bigger picture because the basics are automatic. Your mind is free to notice more. You can adjust, adapt, and improve without losing your rhythm.

Think about learning to play an instrument. At first, it feels like every part of you is out of sync. Your fingers don't move fast enough. You press the wrong keys. Your timing is off. You sound nothing like the music in your head.

Keep Growing

But with practice, it changes. Your hands begin to move without overthinking. Your ear guides your rhythm. The awkwardness fades. You can focus on the feel of the piece instead of the mechanics. The technique becomes second nature. The music starts to flow.

The same is true for any skill. Speaking in public. Learning a new language. Cooking a recipe. Handling a difficult conversation. Driving a car in traffic.

The more you practice, the less you have to fight your own hesitation. You start to move without second-guessing yourself. You start to speak without pausing to search for every word. You start to trust your timing, your touch, your choices.

Each repetition builds a little more confidence.

Each attempt feels a little smoother than the last. What once felt awkward begins to feel natural. The steps that seemed heavy start to carry their own rhythm. Over time, the hesitation fades and is replaced with a quiet certainty that you can do it. And the more you keep going, the more that certainty spreads into other parts of your life. You begin to trust yourself, not because you are perfect, but because you have proven you will keep showing up.

Practice is not just about getting it right once.

It is about getting it right often enough that it becomes the way you do it every time.

When you stop practicing too soon, you keep some of the awkwardness. You keep the hesitation. You leave yourself in the halfway stage where you know the basics but still have to work hard to use them.

Practicing until it is natural removes that struggle.

It smooths out the rough edges. It takes away the awkward pauses and the clumsy mistakes that come from uncertainty. It gives you a foundation you can rely on without thinking. One that holds steady.

But steady is not the same as perfect.

It doesn't mean you will never make a mistake. It means you can move forward with confidence, knowing you can recover quickly if something goes wrong. It means you can keep going without losing your rhythm.

It means steady. It means reliable. It means you can do it under pressure because you have done it so many times before. You are not depending on a lucky moment. You are depending on habit.

The more you practice, the deeper that habit goes.

This is why professionals keep practicing long after they are good at something. A musician rehearses the same songs hundreds of times. An athlete runs the same drills every day. A chef makes the same dish over and over until they can do it with their eyes closed. They are not doing it because they forgot how. They are doing it because they know the value of keeping it natural.

There is a kind of freedom that comes with this level of practice.

When the basics are automatic, you can be more creative. You can make small changes on the fly without worrying that you will throw yourself off. You can handle surprises without losing control because the foundation is already solid.

You have space in your mind for new ideas because you are not using all your energy just to keep up. You can look ahead instead of only focusing on the next step. You can notice opportunities you would have missed if all your effort was spent on holding things together.

Think of a speaker who knows their material so well they do not need notes. They can focus on their audience instead of reading from a page. They can adjust their tone, tell a story, or answer a question without getting lost. That ease only comes from practice until it's natural.

Practice also changes how you feel about the skill. At first, you might dread it. It feels clumsy. Awkward. Hard to get through. You second-guess yourself. You wonder if you are cut out for it at all.

But with enough repetition, you start to enjoy it. You look forward to it. The fear fades because you have proof that you can do it.

Sometimes you will not even notice the exact moment when it becomes natural. There is no announcement. No sign telling you that you have arrived.

One day you will realize you are not thinking about it anymore. You're just doing it. The steps happen in the right order. Your hands or your words move at the right pace. It feels smooth in a way it never did before.

What once took all your focus now happens almost without effort. That is when you know the practice has worked.

And that's the point.

The goal is to practice past the stage of thinking, "I hope I can do this," and into the stage of, "I know I can."

This takes patience.

It takes doing the same thing again and again, even when it feels boring. It takes reminding yourself that you are not just repeating for the sake of it. You are laying down the pathways that will make it easier later.

There is a difference between practicing and just doing something a lot. You can repeat the same action hundreds of times and never get better if you are not paying attention.

Practice is deliberate. It is paying attention to what works and what doesn't. It is adjusting as you go. It is making small improvements each time.

It is like cooking the same recipe again and again. You don't just throw the ingredients together and hope for the best. You notice what works. You adjust the timing, the seasoning, the heat. Each time, the result gets a little better.

Without that attention, repetition can turn into a habit of doing it the wrong way.

So while you practice, stay mindful. Pay attention to what is improving, even if it's only a small change. Notice what feels smoother than last time. Notice where you still hesitate, where your movements slow down or your thoughts get stuck.

Look for the small details you can adjust. It might be the way you position your hands, the order you take the steps, the pace you speak, or the timing of when you start. These details may seem minor in the moment, but they are what take you from awkward to natural. They are the difference between doing something and doing it well.

The process is not always exciting, but it's worth it. Repetition may feel dull in the moment, but it is laying down strength you cannot see yet. Every round of practice is another brick in the foundation that will hold you up later.

When you can do something naturally, it gives you confidence. It means you can step into a situation and trust yourself. It means you can handle pressure without falling apart. It means you have prepared yourself for the moment when it matters most.

So keep going.

Practice past the point of getting it right once. Do it again until you can get it right without thinking about every step. Do it until you can start in the middle and still find your way to the end. Do it until it becomes second nature, even when you are tired, distracted, or under pressure.

Keep Growing

Practice past the point of it feeling like work.

Practice until it feels like second nature.

That is when it becomes yours.

That is common sense.

Connect the Dots

Doing teaches you the basics. But learning does not stop there. Experience is only the first step. Even mastering something leaves room for improvement. What makes it powerful is how you connect what you learn.

Learning is not just about collecting information. It is about making connections. That's the part most people forget. They read the book, watch the video, take the course, and walk away with a head full of facts that never really come together. They gather the pieces but never build anything with them.

Growth happens when those pieces start to link.

Something you heard last week finally makes sense because of something you saw today. A conversation from six months ago clicks into place with an idea you just wrote down. A mistake you made in one part of your life helps you dodge a bigger one somewhere else. That's how it works. Quietly. Suddenly. And then it sticks.

Those moments don't feel dramatic. They are not loud. They are often quiet shifts in perspective. But they matter. Because when you connect the dots, you stop treating learning like a storage game and start using it like a toolbox.

That's the difference. Some people collect dots. Others connect them.

Connecting the dots is how you turn input into insight. It is how you move from just knowing things to actually using them. And it's one of the simplest, most powerful habits you can build into your life.

Think about how many dots you already have.

Keep Growing

You have read things. You have seen things. You have messed up and learned lessons the hard way. You have heard advice that made sense but did not fully land until later. Your life is full of moments, details, stories, and truths that are just sitting there waiting to be connected.

Sometimes the link is obvious.

You learn a new skill and immediately use it at work. You read something that helps you explain an idea more clearly. You remember a quote at just the right moment.

Other times the link shows up in places you did not expect.

A lesson from your high school coach now guides how you lead a team. The rhythm you picked up in music shows up in how you present ideas. Your eye for detail in photography helps you catch mistakes in spreadsheets. Different worlds. Same mind. All connected.

That's what happens when you build the habit of connecting the dots. You start seeing links where you never looked for them before.

This is how creativity works too.

Most creative breakthroughs are not about creating something from nothing. They are about combining things in a new way. The chef who draws inspiration from architecture. The designer who borrows from nature. The entrepreneur who copies a system from one industry and uses it in another.

When you connect ideas across different areas of your life, you give yourself an edge. You think in ways other people don't. You see patterns others miss.

You start to understand that the value of learning is not just in knowing more. It is in seeing how it all fits together.

A person who connects the dots well often seems quick on their feet. But it's not about being fast. It is about having a mental library of links they can reach for.

People who connect dots are not necessarily smarter. They are just better at spotting familiar patterns in new places.

So how do you build this habit?

Start by asking simple questions.

What does this remind me of?

Where have I seen this before?

Is there anything I already know that could help me here?

Does this connect to something I have been struggling with?

Could I use this idea in a different part of my life?

These questions help you pull threads between the things you already know. They help you build a kind of internal map, where lessons in one area light up connections in others.

Write them down. Keep a page in your journal or a note on your phone called "Connections." When two ideas click together, jot it down. It might not feel like much at the time. But those little links add up. Over time, they become the foundation for clearer, sharper thinking.

You can even keep a running list of "unexpected overlaps." A quote from a novel that helped you solve a business problem. A childhood game that taught you how to read people. A YouTube video that gave you a better way to teach your kids something. These moments are gold. The more you notice them, the more they show up.

You will also start noticing more during conversations. Someone shares a story, and instead of thinking, "That was interesting," you start thinking, "That reminds me of..." or "That could actually apply to..."

Keep Growing

This habit makes your mind more flexible. You stop looking at things in isolation. You begin to see how everything is connected.

Here is the mistake most people make.

They think the answer is always more input. They think the problem is that they need to read another book, take another course, listen to another podcast. But often, they already have what they need. They just have not connected it yet.

It is like having a bunch of puzzle pieces and never trying to fit them together.

More information is not always the answer. Sometimes what you need is to step back and look at what you already know from a different angle.

Reflection does that. It gives your brain space to sort through what it has collected and make sense of it.

Even five minutes of quiet thinking can help you notice something new. A short walk. A slow shower. A quiet moment before bed. These are often the moments when dots begin to connect. Your brain keeps working even when you are not actively trying.

That's why ideas often come when you are doing something else entirely. Washing dishes. Folding laundry. Driving with the radio off.

It is not magic. It is your mind finally having room to breathe.

When you step back, the dots start linking on their own.

Another way to connect the dots is by mixing your inputs.

If you only ever read about one topic, you will only see one kind of pattern. But if you expose yourself to different fields, different voices, different styles of thinking, your brain starts to cross-pollinate.

A book on biology helps you understand group behavior in

business.

A documentary about sports coaching changes how you give feedback to your team.

A poem gives you better words to describe your emotions.

A recipe teaches you patience and timing that shows up in how you run meetings.

These unexpected bridges become powerful tools. They give you an advantage because most people never make those connections. They stay in their lane. You start linking the lanes.

And that is where the real growth happens.

You do not need to become an expert in everything. You just need to be open to pulling ideas across boundaries. Take a lesson from one world and bring it into another. That single habit can make you more adaptable, more creative, and more valuable. In work, in relationships, and in how you think through problems.

This also helps in solving problems.

When you are stuck, you can look to another area for ideas.

Maybe a system that works in your hobby could fix something in your job. Maybe a lesson from travel applies to your parenting. Maybe a skill from gardening teaches you patience in business.

The more dots you connect, the more options you see.

Instead of getting stuck in one way of thinking, you start seeing new paths forward. You become more creative, more adaptable, and more effective. You stop focusing on what blocks you and start noticing what connects. That shift trains your mind to see the links instead of dead ends.

And here's the surprising part: you don't always need a brand-new idea. You just need to spot the link that moves an old idea into a new place. A small shift in context can turn something ordinary into something powerful.

The truth is, most people have more knowledge than they realize.

They just have not turned it into wisdom yet.

Wisdom comes from reflection. From synthesis. From seeing how your experiences fit together and what they add up to.

It doesn't take a genius to do this. It just takes attention. It takes the willingness to pause and ask, *What does this mean for me?* or *Where else does this apply?*

Even if you never write it down, just having that internal dialogue changes how your brain works. You begin to notice the familiar inside the unfamiliar. You begin to think not just vertically, but sideways, across domains, across roles, across time.

You already have the dots.

Now build the habit of connecting them.

That is how you grow.

That is common sense.

Seek Feedback Instead of Praise

Praise feels good.

It gives you a boost, a short burst of approval, a moment where you feel seen. A compliment can brighten your day. It reminds you that what you did mattered to someone.

Praise is satisfying in the moment.

But praise, on its own, will not help you grow. It tells you that someone liked the result, but it doesn't tell you what to repeat, what to change, or how to take it further.

Feedback will.

Praise tells you that someone liked what you did. It is a sign that your effort was noticed and appreciated. It can confirm that something worked well.

Feedback tells you how to do it better next time. It points to the details that could be clearer, stronger, or more effective. It gives you direction for what to keep and what to adjust.

Praise is about the past. It looks back at what has already happened.

Feedback is about the future. It gives you something you can use going forward. It gives you direction, not just judgment. It helps you to advance.

If you only chase praise, you will start shaping your actions around getting it. You might avoid challenges because they carry the risk of making mistakes. You might stick to what you already know because it feels safe.

And safe can be the enemy of progress.

Keep Growing

Feedback works differently.

It pushes you into places you have not yet mastered. It challenges you to look at your work from another angle. It shows you where you can improve, whether that means fixing a flaw, refining a detail, or rethinking your approach.

Feedback points out the small adjustments that can make a big difference. It highlights the parts that are unclear, unnecessary, or could be done in a better way.

Sometimes it confirms that what you did worked well. Not because someone is trying to flatter you, but because they can explain why it worked. They can tell you what made it effective and why it had the result it did.

That "why" is valuable. It is something you can repeat, build on, and use to create consistent results in the future.

Seeking feedback means inviting honesty.

That can be uncomfortable.

It is not easy to hear where you fell short. It is not easy to learn that something you thought was great could have been better. But those moments are where growth lives.

You can ask for feedback in small ways.

"What could I do differently next time?"

"Was there anything unclear?"

"Is there something I should focus on improving?"

The more specific your question, the more useful the answer will be. If you ask something general, you will usually get a general response. A vague "What do you think?" often leads to a vague "Looks good."

And "looks good" will not make you better. It gives you a nice moment of approval but no map for what to do next. It doesn't tell you what to change, what to improve, or what to do again next time.

When you ask for detail, you give the other person something to work with. That's when their answer can actually help you grow.

Not all feedback will be good feedback.

Some will be vague. Some will be based on personal preference. Some will not apply to your situation at all. You do not have to accept every suggestion, but you should think about each one before deciding whether to use it.

Sometimes feedback will clash. One person will tell you to go in one direction, another will tell you to go the opposite way. In those moments, you still get to decide what fits best for you. The value is not in following every piece of advice, but in considering it.

When you respond well to feedback, you make it easier for people to give it to you in the future. If you get defensive or dismissive, they will hold back. They will not want to risk upsetting you or wasting their effort.

But if you thank them and show you are listening, they will feel that their input matters. They will be more willing to share what they see next time. Over time, that steady flow of honest feedback becomes one of your best tools for improving.

That does not mean you have to agree with everything you hear. It just means you respect the effort it took for someone to be honest with you.

Feedback is not a personal attack.

Feedback is a tool.

It is something you can use to close the gap between where you are and where you want to be. It helps you take what is already working and make it stronger. It helps you find what is holding you back

Keep Growing

and remove it. It gives you a clearer path toward the results you want.

Sometimes feedback is exactly what you expected. Other times it will surprise you. It might reveal blind spots you didn't know you had. It might confirm a strength you weren't sure about. It might show you that something small you have been overlooking is more important than you thought.

And while praise fades quickly, good feedback can stay with you for years. You can return to it long after the moment has passed. You can read it again, think about it again, and see new ways to apply it. You can keep coming back to it, adjusting and improving over time, each time getting a little closer to the result you want.

If you start asking for feedback regularly, you will notice something. Your focus shifts. You stop aiming only to be liked, and you start aiming to be better. You value the truth over comfort. You care more about improvement than applause.

It also sharpens your work. Instead of guessing what works, you are getting real information from people who see your blind spots. Instead of hoping you are on the right track, you can check and adjust along the way. You are not just working harder. You are working smarter, with direction.

That shift changes how you see feedback. You stop fearing it and start looking for it. You take on things you might have avoided before, not because you expect perfection, but because you know the feedback will help you grow. You see it as part of the process, not a judgment.

Feedback also strengthens relationships.

When you show that you can handle constructive criticism, people trust you more. They know they can be honest with you without hurting the relationship. And when they see you using their input, they feel that their voice matters. They are wiling to provide more feedback.

Sometimes, the hardest feedback to hear is the most valuable.

If it stings, it is worth asking yourself why. Is it because the person was unfair, or because they pointed out something you already suspected was true? If it is the second, you might have just been handed the exact key you need to improve.

None of this means you have to stop enjoying praise. It is nice to be appreciated. It is nice to know your work had a positive impact. Praise can be motivating, but it should not be the only thing you are working for.

If you focus only on praise, you can end up stuck in a loop of doing what is safe and familiar. If you focus on feedback, you open yourself to growth you cannot get any other way.

So the next time you finish a project, give a presentation, or try something new, do not just ask, "What did you like?" That question might bring a few compliments, but it will not give you much to work with.

Ask instead, "What would make this better?" That question invites detail. It opens the door for specific suggestions you can actually use. It tells the other person you are serious about improving, not just collecting praise.

Do that often enough, and you will stop fearing feedback. The discomfort will fade as you get used to hearing it. You will start looking forward to it because you will know it's helping you improve. You will start seeing it as a shortcut to where you want to be, a way to move forward faster than you could on your own.

Praise is nice.

But feedback lasts.

Seek feedback instead of praise.

That is common sense.

Teach What You Know

If you want to understand something better, try teaching it.

Teaching is not just for classrooms.

It happens in everyday life, often without you noticing. It is showing a friend how to fix a dripping tap instead of quietly doing it for them. It is walking a coworker through a process they have never used before so next time they can do it on their own. It is explaining to a neighbour how to care for a plant you have kept alive for years, sharing the small habits that make the difference.

It might be showing a child how to tie their shoes or ride a bike. It might be helping a family member set up a new phone or guiding someone through a recipe you have cooked dozens of times. It might be offering a small tip to someone just starting a hobby you have enjoyed for years.

These moments do not look like formal lessons, but they are teaching just as much. You are passing on knowledge, guiding someone through a skill, and helping them understand something they did not know before.

When you teach, you pass on something that took you time to learn. You hand over the shortcuts you discovered. You share the little mistakes to avoid. You make someone else's path a little smoother than yours was.

And in the process, you often see your own knowledge in a new way.

Questions from others can make you think about things you take for granted. They can reveal gaps in your knowledge. They can push you to find better examples, clearer explanations, and simpler ways to show what you mean.

Sometimes you realize you know more than you thought. Sometimes you realize you know less. Both discoveries are valuable.

Teaching also strengthens your memory. The more you recall and use information, the more firmly it stays with you. When you teach something, you are retrieving it from your memory, shaping it into words, and applying it in real time. That process reinforces the knowledge in a way that passive review never can.

You do not have to be an expert to teach.

You just have to be a step ahead of the person you are helping. You might only know the basics, but to someone starting from zero, those basics are valuable. Your experience might be exactly what they need, even if you still have more to learn yourself.

Sometimes it's even better when you are not too far ahead. You still remember what it feels like to be new. You remember the early challenges and the simple mistakes. You remember what confused you and what finally made it click.

That memory can make you a better teacher than someone so advanced they have forgotten what it was like to start. But you still remember the struggle. You know which parts felt confusing and where people tend to get stuck. You know what helped you move forward, and that makes you better at guiding someone else through it.

Teaching builds connection.

It is more than just passing along information. It is a moment where you give part of yourself, your time, your focus, and your patience to someone else.

Teaching also creates trust.

The person you are helping sees that you are willing to share what you know without holding back. They see that you care enough to make sure they understand.

It shows that you are willing to give your time and attention to help someone else grow. It is an act of generosity, and people remember it. They remember who took the time to guide them. They remember who made a challenge feel less overwhelming. They remember who believed they could do it before they believed it themselves.

And there is another benefit. When you teach, you are forced to organize your own thinking. You cannot hand someone a tangled ball of ideas and expect them to make sense of it. You have to lay it out in a way that is clear, step by step, so they can follow along.

It is like cleaning a cluttered drawer before showing someone where to find something. In the process of making it easier for them, you also make it easier for yourself. You can see what you have, what you are missing, and what doesn't belong.

That order and clarity often carries over into other parts of your work and life. You start breaking down your own work more methodically. You start explaining things to yourself the same way you would explain them to someone else. The habit of making things clear for others makes them clearer for you.

Sometimes teaching inspires you to keep learning.

You see how much there is still to explore. You find yourself wanting to answer questions you could not answer before. You look for better ways to explain things next time.

You also get to see the impact of what you know.

Watching someone succeed because of something you shared is deeply satisfying. You see the moment it clicks, the shift from confusion to confidence. You see them take what you offered, run with it, and make it their own. There is a quiet joy in knowing you helped light the path.

Teach What You Know

Their progress becomes part of your own story. Every time they use that skill or that knowledge, a small part of it traces back to you. It is a quiet reminder that what you know has value, not just for you, but for the people around you.

Teaching can take many forms.

It can be formal, like leading a workshop or giving a talk. It can be informal, like helping a friend cook a new recipe or showing a child how to ride a bike. It can happen in a single conversation or over months of mentoring.

What matters is the sharing.

Every time you teach, you keep the knowledge alive.

Information that stays locked in your head doesn't grow. When you share it, you give it the chance to help someone else, and often it comes back to you in a stronger form.

Sometimes the person you teach will take what you showed them and build on it. They will make small changes that fit their style. They will add their own skill, their own way of doing things, their own understanding.

Over time, it becomes something slightly different from what you first taught. And that is a good thing. It means they have made it their own. They have taken what you gave them and adapted it to fit their voice, their experience, their way of doing things.

Then they will pass it on again. They will teach someone else, who might add their own changes too. The idea keeps moving, changing a little each time, but still carrying a piece of what you first shared. What you gave continues to echo, even as it grows into something new.

That's how knowledge spreads. One person to another. One small step at a time.

If you are unsure whether you are ready to teach, start small. Show

Keep Growing

someone a tip that has worked for you. Explain one step of a process instead of the whole thing. Share a single example that makes a concept clearer.

The more you do it, the easier it becomes. You learn which explanations work best. You learn where people tend to get stuck. You learn how to adapt your approach to different personalities and learning styles.

Over time, teaching can become part of how you think. You start to see lessons everywhere, not just for yourself, but for others. You recognize moments when a small piece of advice could make a big difference.

Teaching is not about showing off.

It is not about proving that you know more than someone else. It is about helping them move forward from where they are now.

When you teach, you are not just giving information. You are giving confidence. You are showing someone that they can do something they could not do before. That confidence can stay with them long after the specific lesson is over.

And you get something in return. You get the satisfaction of making a difference. You get the growth that comes from explaining and answering questions. You get the reminder that knowledge is most valuable when it is shared.

You can spend a lifetime collecting what you know.

Or you can pass it on and watch it grow in other people's hands.

Teach what you know.

It is good for you.

It is good for them.

That is common sense.

Look Back to Move Forward

It is tempting to always be thinking about what comes next. The next task. The next project. The next goal. Forward is where the progress is, after all. At least, that is what we tell ourselves.

But progress does not come only from moving ahead. It also comes from stopping long enough to see where you have been.

Looking back is not about living in the past. It is about learning from it. It is about finding the patterns, the lessons, and the reminders that make your next step wiser than your last.

When you take a moment to look back, you see more than just the big milestones. You notice the smaller choices that got you there. You see the detours you did not expect but still managed to navigate. You see where you hesitated and where you acted too quickly. You see what worked and what did not.

Reflection turns experience into insight.

Without reflection, you are just stacking up days. You wake up, move through your routine, and cross things off the list. But you are not seeing the bigger picture. The days blur together. You feel busy, maybe even accomplished. Still, you cannot tell if you are getting closer to what matters.

You keep moving, but without direction. It is like walking through fog. One foot, then the next. No sense of whether you are heading forward or backward. Until you pause to look back, you have no way to adjust your course.

Think about the last time you had a setback. In the moment, it probably felt frustrating or even pointless. But looking back, you might see that it taught you something you could not have learned any other way.

Keep Growing

Maybe you lost a job and it forced you to reassess what you really wanted from your work. At the time, it felt like a disaster. But in hindsight, it pushed you into a role that suited you better. Or maybe you missed a deadline because you underestimated the time a task would take. It was embarrassing then, but it taught you to build more margin into your schedule.

Now think about the last time you succeeded at something important. In the moment, you probably celebrated and then quickly moved on to the next challenge.

But look back now. You can see the hours of practice that built your skill. You can see the setbacks that forced you to adjust. You can see the habits that carried you through when motivation faded. Success rarely comes from the final push. It comes from the groundwork you hardly noticed at the time.

Maybe you finally ran that half marathon. The race was exciting, but the real win was the months of early mornings you got up to train. Or maybe you nailed a big presentation at work. The applause was nice, but it was the hours of preparation and small practice runs that made it go smoothly.

Looking back gives you the full picture. It is the difference between glancing at a single puzzle piece and stepping back to see the whole image. Suddenly the piece makes sense. You can see where it fits and why it matters.

Without reflection, you risk repeating the same mistakes.

You move forward without noticing what went wrong. You keep doing what you've always done, hoping this time it will work out differently.

But hope is not a strategy.

If you never pause to ask what didn't work, you never see the pattern. You keep following the same routine, not realizing the routine itself is the problem.

With reflection, you start to see the patterns in your own life. The choices that consistently help you and the ones that always seem to backfire. The people who bring out your best and the situations that drag you down. You see what you want to do differently, and you see what you want to keep exactly the same.

This is not about overthinking every decision. It is about giving yourself a few moments of honesty.

Ask yourself simple questions:

What went well this week?

What did not?

What will I do differently next time?

These questions work in any situation. After a big project at work. After a personal challenge. After a difficult conversation. Even at the end of an ordinary week.

Try this: At the end of each week, write down three things. One thing that went well. One thing that didn't. One thing you want to try next week.

Some weeks your notes might be short and simple. "Well: met deadlines. Not well: skipped lunch. Try: block lunch on my calendar." Other times, you might write more. A thought you want to remember. A small win. A problem that keeps coming back.

The point is not to write perfectly. The point is to notice. Over time, those notes start to reveal patterns. You see what strengthens your days and what pulls them apart. You spot the habits that carry you forward and the ones that drain your energy.

And when you look back, the picture is clear. You see problems that once felt overwhelming now handled with ease. You see mistakes that once kept repeating now replaced by better decisions. You see proof of progress, even if it came so slowly you could not see it in the moment. Writing things down turns vague memories into

Keep Growing

solid evidence. It shows you how far you have come and reminds you that growth is happening, even when you are too close to notice it.

We often think progress means moving fast. But speed without clarity is wasted effort. True progress comes from knowing where you have been and where you are going.

If you never stop to reflect, you risk racing in the wrong direction. You might climb hard and climb high, only to find the ladder against the wrong wall.

Reflection is your chance to check the wall before you climb higher.

Sometimes looking back means admitting you made mistakes. That can be uncomfortable. It is easier to push forward and pretend it never happened. But avoiding the lesson means carrying the same weakness into the future. The next time you face a similar challenge, you will be no better prepared to handle it.

When you take the time to face your mistakes, you change the story. A failure becomes a teacher. A mistake becomes a map of what not to do next time. A wrong turn becomes a landmark that keeps you on track in the future.

Looking back can reveal strengths you did not know you had. Maybe you stayed calm in a moment that would have rattled you before. Maybe you found a solution under pressure that showed you just how capable you really are. These moments matter. They are proof that you are growing, even when it doesn't feel like it.

Reflection builds confidence.

Not the loud kind, but the steady kind. The kind that comes from knowing you have been through hard things and handled them. Maybe not perfectly, but with enough clarity and resilience to move forward. That is how trust in yourself is built: through evidence, not wishful thinking.

Reflection is not just about the past. It takes your experiences and shapes them into building blocks for what comes next. It connects where you have been with where you are going.

Sometimes that means repeating what worked. Sometimes it means avoiding what did not. And sometimes it means adjusting, improving, and trying again with a better plan.

You don't need hours of meditation or a complicated journal to do this. You just need to be willing to pause. A walk without your phone. A few quiet minutes before bed. A conversation with someone you trust. The important thing is to make space for it.

Looking back is not weakness. It is not dwelling. It is not slowing down for the sake of it. It is making sure that when you move forward, you are doing it with more knowledge, more clarity, and more purpose than before.

It is like hiking in unfamiliar terrain. If you never look back, you will have no landmarks to guide you. If you get turned around, you will not remember what the trail looked like from the other direction. By glancing back as you go, you prepare yourself to find the way home if you need to.

Looking back gives you reference points. It gives you markers to navigate by. It keeps you from getting lost in the rush to keep moving.

So before you take your next big step, pause. Look over your shoulder. See what the path behind you can teach you about the path ahead.

Move forward, yes.

But move forward with the confidence that comes from knowing exactly where you have been.

The past is not a weight. It is a guide.

That is common sense.

Don't Be Afraid of Making Mistakes

Mistakes are part of the deal.

You cannot learn without them. You cannot grow without them. Mistakes are built into the process of getting better at anything. Each one brings a lesson, if you are willing to look.

Yet many people hold back because they are afraid of getting something wrong. They delay starting. They overthink every move. They wait until they feel ready, which often means they never begin.

The truth is, you will make mistakes. Everyone does. No matter how careful you are, no matter how much you prepare, some things will not go the way you planned.

The question is not whether you will make mistakes, but what you will do afterward. Will you get stuck replaying them in your head, wishing you could go back? Will you try to hide it and hope no one noticed? Or will you take a clear look at what happened and decide how to do it better next time?

Fear of mistakes can keep you stuck.

It can make you hesitate before trying something new. It can stop you from taking the first step at all.

It can keep you in the safe zone where nothing goes wrong, but nothing improves either. You stay where you already know the outcome, where there are no surprises, but also no growth.

Fear of mistakes can make you aim for safe and small when you are capable of more. You lower your goals so you can be sure of reaching them, even if it means missing the chance to discover what you could really do.

Don't Be Afraid of Making Mistakes

When you are not afraid of mistakes, you give yourself permission to move forward. You take more chances. You try new approaches. You push into areas you have not mastered yet. You open doors that fear would have kept closed.

Some mistakes will be small and easy to fix. You might use the wrong setting on a tool, forget an ingredient in a recipe, or misplace a file. These are small corrections. They are the kind you laugh about later.

Other mistakes feel bigger. You might take on a project and realize you underestimated the time and effort it would take. You might make a choice that costs you money, time, or opportunities. These sting more. They take longer to recover from.

Both have value. Both carry lessons you would not have learned any other way.

Mistakes are not proof that you are failing. They are proof that you are trying. They are a sign that you are stretching beyond what is familiar. They show that you are putting yourself in situations where you cannot be certain of the outcome.

Every skill, every craft, every bit of progress is built on a trail of mistakes. What looks smooth and effortless now was once awkward and full of wrong turns. What feels natural today once felt clumsy and uncertain.

Behind every polished performance is a history of missed steps, failed tries, and lessons learned through persistence. Those early struggles are not wasted. They are the groundwork. Without them, the ease you see now could never exist.

The people you admire for being great at what they do have made more mistakes than you have even attempted yet. They have failed in ways you have not even imagined. They learned by trying, failing, and adjusting until they found what worked. Then they kept adjusting until it worked even better.

Their success is built on the foundation of those mistakes. Without them, they would not have the skill, the confidence, or the knowledge they have today.

Think about learning to walk. As a child, you did not worry about looking foolish when you fell. You stood back up and tried again. If you had been afraid of falling, you would never have learned to walk at all.

The same principle applies to everything you learn later in life. You cannot skip the part where you stumble. You cannot get to confidence without going through uncertainty.

The fear of mistakes often comes from worrying about what others will think. You imagine their eyes on you, waiting for you to slip. You picture the embarrassment of getting it wrong. But the truth is, most people are too caught up in their own challenges to remember yours for long. And the few who do notice, the ones who matter, will understand. They have stumbled too.

They know mistakes are part of learning.

When you are willing to make mistakes, you take away their power over you. You stop letting them control your choices. You stop giving them more weight than they deserve.

Mistakes are just information. They are not a final judgment on your ability or your worth. They are a message about what doesn't work in the way you hoped.

They tell you something about what doesn't work. They highlight the weak spots, the missing steps, or the wrong approach.

They point you toward what might work better next time. Each one is a signpost, showing you where to turn, where to adjust, and where to try again with a different strategy.

The fastest learners are the ones willing to stumble.

They don't wait for perfect conditions. They start, they try, they trip, and they adjust. Every mistake moves them forward. What slows most people down is not failure but the fear of it. Lose that fear, and progress comes quickly.

If you are going to fail, fail fast. Find out quickly what does not work so you can make changes sooner. Every mistake gives you feedback you can use right away.

The fastest learners gather more feedback. They get more practice at recovering. Each time they adjust, they sharpen their instincts and improve their approach. Over time, they build resilience as well as skill, because they have learned how to handle setbacks without losing momentum.

This doesn't mean you should try to be careless. It means you should not let the possibility of getting it wrong keep you from acting at all.

Act. Learn. Adjust.

If you avoid taking action because you might fail, you guarantee that you will not succeed. As Wayne Gretzky once said, you miss one hundred percent of the shots you do not take. If you never speak up because you might say the wrong thing, your voice will never be heard. If you never try something new because you might make a mistake, you will stay exactly where you are.

Sometimes the mistakes you fear the most turn out to be the most useful. They shake up your assumptions. They make you re-examine what you thought you knew. They push you to be more resourceful, creative, and adaptable.

When you make one, don't rush to hide it. Look at it closely. Ask yourself what happened, why it happened, and what you can change. That is how mistakes become stepping stones instead of roadblocks.

You will also find that the more mistakes you make, the less they bother you. You stop treating them like disasters. You start treating

Keep Growing

them like part of the work. You see them for what they are: temporary setbacks on the way to something better.

Don't be afraid of the small mistakes. Don't be afraid of the big ones either. The small ones keep you sharp. The big ones teach you lessons you will never forget.

Fear shrinks your world. Letting go of that fear opens it up again.

So take the shot. Speak up. Pitch the idea. Try the move. Take the leap.

Try the thing you are not quite ready for. Whatever that is. Step into it knowing you might make mistakes. Let yourself get it wrong, and then use what you learn to make it right next time. Each attempt will give you a little more skill, a little more confidence, and a little less fear.

The more you do this, the easier it becomes to start before you feel ready. You stop waiting for perfect preparation and start trusting that you can figure things out as you go.

Mistakes will happen.

They are proof you are moving, learning, and willing to try.

Each one can move you forward, if you let it.

That is how you get better.

That is common sense.

Don't Get Comfortable

Comfort feels good. That's why we like it. It is the familiar chair, the easy routine, the things we already know how to do without thinking too hard. It is safe. It is predictable. It is also where growth quietly comes to a stop.

The problem with comfort is not that it's bad. The problem is that it's easy to stay there too long. You start avoiding the things that make you uncertain. You stop putting yourself in situations where you might fail. You choose the familiar not because it is best, but because it is easiest.

And little by little, you stop learning.

Comfort is a place to rest, not a place to live.

It is where you pause to catch your breath before you take the next step, not where you set up camp. Comfort is meant to be a temporary stop, a place to rest and reset before you head back out into the unknown. If you stay there too long, it stops being rest and starts becoming a barrier.

If you want to keep growing, you have to step outside of what feels safe.

That doesn't always mean taking big, dramatic risks. More often, growth comes from small, deliberate choices that push you just a little beyond your comfort zone. Each stretch builds strength without overwhelming you.

It might be as simple as saying yes to something you have never done before. Enrolling in a class that challenges you. Talking to someone you don't know and seeing where the conversation goes. Trying a new approach when the old one is still "good enough" but no longer inspiring.

These little pushes add up. Each one expands the edges of what feels possible.

The best opportunities in life often hide just outside your comfort zone. They are rarely wrapped in certainty. More often, they come disguised as things that feel inconvenient, intimidating, or uncomfortable.

Think about the last time you did something that scared you a little. Maybe you gave a speech, took on a project you were not sure you could handle, or traveled to a place where you did not speak the language. Chances are, when it was over, you felt stronger. More capable. More alive.

That is the strange thing about discomfort. In the moment, it can feel awkward or even painful. But afterward, it leaves you with something comfort never can: a bigger sense of what you can handle.

When you stretch yourself, you don't just gain a new skill or a new experience. You gain proof that you can stretch. That makes it easier to do it again next time.

Staying too comfortable makes you fragile.

The longer you avoid challenge, the more intimidating it feels. You start to doubt your ability to handle the unexpected. You start building your life around avoiding uncertainty, and in the process, you shrink your world.

On the other hand, when you regularly step into discomfort, you build resilience. You get used to the feeling of not knowing exactly how things will go. You trust yourself to figure it out along the way.

That doesn't mean living in a constant state of stress. You don't need to throw yourself into chaos for the sake of it. It means making sure you are still challenging yourself in ways that matter.

It could be a personal goal. Running a little farther than you have before. Learning a skill that doesn't come naturally.

It could be in your relationships. Having an honest conversation you have been avoiding. Listening to a perspective you disagree with.

It could be at work. Asking for a responsibility that scares you a little. Speaking up in a meeting where you would normally stay quiet.

Each small push expands what feels possible.

The danger is not in taking these steps. The danger is in convincing yourself you do not need to take them anymore. You tell yourself you are "fine where you are." You let your days become predictable, not because you love them that way, but because they require no effort to maintain.

Over time, that predictability stops feeling like peace and starts feeling like being stuck.

Growth doesn't happen automatically. It doesn't show up just because time passes. It happens when you make a choice to stretch. To go somewhere new. To try something unfamiliar. To risk getting it wrong.

You grow by stepping forward, even when you are not sure what comes next. Each time you move into the unknown, you give yourself a chance to find something you could never reach by staying where you are.

It may feel uncomfortable at first. That is often the signal that you are in the right place. That is where growth begins.

The irony is that once you step into the unfamiliar, it eventually becomes comfortable too. That is when you have to push again.

This is the cycle of growth. Step forward. Learn. Adjust. Settle in. Then, before you get too comfortable, step again.

Keep Growing

If you wait until you "feel ready," you will wait forever. Comfort is persuasive. It will always give you reasons to stay. Reasons that sound smart, safe, and responsible. But deep down, you will know they are excuses.

The truth is, you don't grow by staying where everything is easy. Easy feels good, but it keeps you still. It gives you comfort, not progress. You grow by stepping into the moments that make you uncomfortable. The ones that force you to think deeper, try harder, and keep going when you want to quit.

Those moments test you. They show you where your limits actually are. And more often than not, they show you that you can go further than you ever believed.

It is like lifting weights. If you keep lifting the same amount forever, your muscles stop getting stronger. You only build strength by gradually increasing the challenge. The same is true for your skills, your mindset, and your life.

You don't need to chase discomfort just to prove something.

Life will hand you enough hard things on its own.

What matters is noticing when comfort turns into something else. When rest becomes routine. When routine becomes a cage. When the days start to blur and nothing challenges you anymore. That is the moment to pay attention.

When that happens, you know it's time to move. Not in a frantic rush, but with a clear choice to step into something that stretches you again. It might be a small step or a big one, but either way, it's a step toward growth.

This doesn't mean you will always feel ready. In fact, if you are waiting to feel ready, you are waiting too long. The moment you feel too comfortable is the moment you should look for your next challenge. Growth lives just beyond that edge of comfort.

The best part is that once you make a habit of stepping outside your comfort zone, it stops being so intimidating. You start to see discomfort as a sign you are on the right track. You learn to trust that you can handle it, because you have before.

And over time, you will notice something else. Life gets bigger. You meet people you never would have met. You discover interests you did not know you had. You find opportunities you could not have imagined from inside your familiar routine.

Comfort is sweet in small doses. It is a reward. A rest stop. But it's not where you are meant to stay forever.

You are meant to keep moving. To keep learning. To keep growing.

So enjoy comfort when it comes, but don't let it hold you still. Take the next step, even if it feels awkward. Especially if it feels awkward.

Comfort will always be there when you return.

Growth will not wait around.

That is common sense.

Before You Go

Before You Go

By now, you have seen what this book is really about. It is not a list of rules or a system to master. It is not about chasing perfection or reinventing your life from the ground up. It is about remembering what you already know and giving yourself the courage to live by it.

Common sense is not glamorous.

It will not grab headlines or impress a crowd. It is not a hidden formula or a clever trick waiting to be unlocked. It is the kind of wisdom that lives in plain sight, so ordinary that it is easy to overlook. People often dismiss it as too simple to matter. The truth is, common sense is simple. But simple does not mean easy.

You already know the basics. Get enough sleep, but late nights still win more often than they should. Listen more than you speak, but your temper still slips through. Take small, steady steps, but you still wait for the perfect moment to begin.

The real test is not knowledge. The real test is action. It is doing what you already know, and then doing it again tomorrow, and the day after that.

That's why common sense matters. It is the bridge between what you know and how you live. It reminds you that small, thoughtful actions, repeated over time, create more change than big ideas that never leave your head.

The world will try to pull you away from that. It rewards speed, noise, and shortcuts. It will whisper that success depends on some secret method you have not yet discovered. But the truth is, there are no hidden keys. The basics you already know, practiced with honesty and steadiness, are what move you forward.

You don't need secret formulas or complex methods. You need the willingness to keep showing up and to practice simple things until they become part of you.

And here is the good news: you already have what it takes.

You don't need permission, special tools, or a perfect plan.

You only need to choose one small action and begin. Pick something you care about. Try it tomorrow. Then try it again the next day. Stack those small wins until they become a rhythm.

You don't have to apply everything at once.

Life is not a race to master everything. Even a few steady changes will make more difference than trying to do it all and burning out.

Maybe you start with one habit. Maybe you focus on one mindset shift. Maybe you choose a relationship to invest in more deeply. Whatever you choose, give it a fair try. See what happens. Small steps can open doors you never expected.

You will not get it right every time. You will forget. You will get distracted. You will fall back into old habits. That is normal. The point is not to never fail. The point is to notice when you drift and return without turning it into a drama. Each return is proof that you are still in the game.

Don't think of this as climbing to the top of a ladder. Think of it as moving through a loop that you circle again and again. Each time you come back, you will see something new. Some lessons will fit your life today. Others will matter more tomorrow. The cycle itself is the practice.

In the end, the biggest changes will not come from what you learn here. They will come from what you choose to live. The difference between a book you read and a life you shape is action. One thoughtful step forward is worth more than a hundred clever ideas left unused.

So let this book be a reminder, not a checklist.

Use it as a touchstone when life feels too fast, too complicated, or too uncertain.

Return to the basics. Choose presence over hurry. Choose honesty over noise. Choose one small step instead of waiting for the perfect leap.

If you remember only one thing, remember this: life changes when you practice the basics. Not once, not sometimes, but every day. It is not theory. It is not wishful thinking. It is the quiet proof that shows up in your actions, your habits, and your results.

Step by step, the things you repeat shape the life you live. That is how progress is made. That is how character is built.

Keep moving forward.

Keep your eyes open.

Keep building habits that make life steadier, kinder, and more meaningful.

That is common sense.

www.ingramcontent.com/pod-product-compliance
Lightning Source LLC
Chambersburg PA
CBHW071151070526
44584CB00019B/2753